Love Magic

Love Magic

MARINA MEDICI

PHOTOGRAPHY BY

Bruno Kortenhorst
&
Carlos Rios

SIMON & SCHUSTER

LONDON·SYDNEY·NEW YORK·TOKYO·SINGAPORE·TORONTO

SIMON &
SCHUSTER

Simon & Schuster
First published in Great Britain by
Simon & Schuster Ltd in 1994
A Paramount Communications Company

A LABYRINTH BOOK

© 1994 by Labyrinth Publishing (UK) Ltd
Text © 1994 by Marina Medici
Original Illustrations © 1994 by Labyrinth Publishing (UK) Ltd
Original Photographs © 1994 by Bruno Kortenhorst and Carlos Rios

Simon and Schuster Ltd
West Garden Place
Kendal Street London W2 2AQ

Simon and Schuster of Australia Pty Ltd Sydney

A CIP catalogue record for this book is
available from the British Library
ISBN 0-671-71208-X
1 3 5 7 9 10 8 6 4 2

LOVE MAGIC was produced by Labyrinth Publishing (UK) Ltd
Design by Carmen Strider
Typesetting by Carmen Strider
Printed and bound in Singapore by Craft Print Pte Ltd

For Etta, who taught me well.

Contents

This book is for lovers. Not for witches, magicians or shamans — only for lovers. To be in love is magic, and magic serves the purpose of helping us to fall in love and stay in love.

It is sad that this fundamental principle (magic equals love) has been forgotten, and lovers all over the world are running to all kinds of psychologists and therapists — if they haven't given up altogether — when all that is needed is a little magic, and everything can be well again.

It seems simple enough, except that there is a snag. For the magic to work, we have to believe in it. And that is not always such an easy thing to do. The biggest obstacle to believing in something is seriousness. If we are "serious" then there is immediately a "problem." So if you have difficulty in believing, simply pretend to believe. Forget seriousness and enjoy the game — you might get the Moon phase wrong or burn the pot, but by starting out playfully you will come a lot closer to the real essence of Love Magic.

PART 1

Innocence

The Garden of Love

Cupid is always depicted as an infant, and even though
we might sometimes feel that his innocence leads
him into mischief, we can rarely resist the power of his
arrows of love.

We are born in love.

Watch a baby, see the bliss in his eyes when he is just there, in the present moment, and there are no disturbances (when he is not wet or hungry or afraid). See the total, uncomplicated trust that he is able to develop with his main caretaker (in most cases the mother).

The child does not come into the world "in love" with his mother, but she is "in love" with him, and it is with this love that she receives the person closest to her. Growing up in this world that has become so oblivious to magic, the child sooner or later forgets his inborn capacity for innocence, trust, and love. But this capacity is not erased, it is only forgotten. It remains at the core of his being, waiting to be rediscovered.

Magicians throughout the ages have always been those people who have found a key that takes them back to that core, for this is the place where all magic begins.

In this book we will learn the art of "remembering" the love of innocent childhood, and then we will learn how to create a space around us and inside us so that we can nourish and protect what we have rediscovered.

Moreover we will learn how to clean out the weeds growing around love — the jealousies, the fears, the misunderstandings — clearing the way for the magic of sharing, and delighting in the fusion of hearts and bodies.

The flame of a candle serves as both a helper in enabling
us to focus, and as a doorway to relaxing and letting go
of our everyday worries.

Beginning at The Beginning: The Basic Love Ritual

The following ritual helps us to get in touch with the love within. It is the most important, basic step of Love Magic learning. Through this ritual we are reintroduced to ourselves as creatures of love, and find the source from where all our love can be graced by the presence of magic.

It begins like this:

Choose a comfortable space in your house. (Later we will see how to create a special space for Love Magic, but for the time being simply use a familiar area that you normally use for relaxing.) Make sure that it is clean and uncluttered, and that you will not be disturbed.

After cleansing yourself (see "Preparation and Purification for Magic Practice," page 68) sit comfortably, in a relaxed position. All lights should be extinguished except for the flicker of a white candle.

Now gaze at the candle, at the same time allowing yourself to become aware of your breathing. Don't change the breathing, just watch it as it comes and goes. You may feel like taking a deep breath — and if you do, you may notice that the whole body relaxes a little as you exhale.

If you feel like closing your eyes at any point, this is fine.

Now feel the contact of your body with the floor, the cushion or the chair where you are sitting. Check out your shoulders — are they tense? Let them relax. Make whatever adjustments you need to make so that your body is comfortable, and then go back to being aware of your breathing.

Now shift your attention to the base of your spine.

Some people will easily feel that there is an "energy" gathered here. They may feel it as heat, or tingling, or a sense of spaciousness, or whatever. It is different, for different people.

Others may not feel anything at first, and in fact this is quite common. In that case, you can use your imagination to help you. Imagine that you are "breathing into" that space at the base of your spine, and that your breath is bringing life and energy to that place, making it alive and full, like a bubbling spring, ready to overflow.

At this point, I want to mention an alternative in case you find that this imagery of the

Energy moves naturally upward. All you have to do is to "feel" it from the base of your spine, gently filling your whole body. With practice in Love Magic your capacity to let it rise higher and higher will increase.

base of the spine doesn't work for you. And that is to begin with the energy at your sex center, the place where your body first feels "turned on" by a sexual partner. This is quite easy for most people and in fact, physiologically, it is basically the same place as the base of the spine. The danger with this imagery, however, is that it is very easy to get lost in sexual fantasies, which is not the point of this ritual. So if you find this easier, by all means use it. But stay alert and don't let your mind wander into passionate scenes!

Now — all you have to do is to "feel" the rising of your energy from the base of your spine, gently flowing upwards.

You can use any imagery which for you has the power to "lift." It could be flowers — roses for example, beautifully colored, delicately scented roses. It could be the vision of a mountain spring, the pure crystal water emerging from the solid rocks. It could be an image of a vast, blue sky. Find inside you the scents of earth and humid air or the peaceful sounds and murmurs of water. Let the images, or just the physical sensations of flowing and aliveness, carry the energy from the source upwards, filling all the little crevices in your spine. Let it spill over into your belly, and spread upwards from there into your solar plexus and into your heart. Keep the connection with the source, though, this is important. This energy is a filling up and overflowing, not some little creature that travels around in your body like a space ship!

Be playful with it, see how far you can get it to rise before you lose the connection with the source. As you practice, you will find that it rises higher and higher, and spreads throughout your whole body, flowing out into your arms and legs and filling you up to the top of your head. It can even start filling the space around you, so that the whole room is alive and pulsing with energy.

At the end of the ritual — when you have "lost the thread" or feel like you have "had enough" for now or can't contain anymore, gently turn your attention back to watching your breathing, and rest there for a while. Open your eyes and look at the candle as you do this. And then, when you feel ready, let your energy do what it wants to do — laugh, dance, cry, go for a walk, have an ice cream, or take a nap — whatever it wants to do.

Many Eastern spiritual traditions have long recognized
that sexual energy is not sinful, but a powerful force that
can be used for personal transformation.

Rising in Love

It sounds very simple, and in fact it is more than simple, for this feeling of rising energy is our own natural happiness and liveliness. We were born with it, it is the source of "being in love." But for many people this simple imagining can prove extremely difficult.

The sad truth is that we have spent much of our lives doing the reverse of allowing our energy to rise — instead "pushing down" or "sitting on" this spring of life inside ourselves. When we are children we learn to "sit still and be quiet," when we are teenagers we learn to "stay cool." From the time we are able to crawl on our hands and knees we are taught to constrict our own vitality in order to conform to the wishes and expectations of others. We allow so many wounds to close our hearts, thus clamping down on the spring of life.

But it is easily possible to reactivate the positive side of our natures by allowing the energy of love to move upwards through the body according to this method. It is possible, in the process, that we will encounter the feelings connected with these old wounds that we have gathered from repressing our own energy. It is easy to be frightened of changing, of appearing to leave ourselves unprotected. But in the world of magic there is no cause for fear. Ancient wisdom, rituals, magic stones, scents and the help of our lovers are all available to protect our innocence and help us to heal.

PART II

Moon Love...

Below: The Egyptian god Thoth, whose wisdom brings
light into the darkness as the daylight falls away.
Opposite: A telescope or good pair of binoculars can bring
the magic of the Moon so close you feel you can touch it.

One of the first tasks for the Love Magician is to get acquainted with the Moon — for without the Moon there would be no love and no Love Magic. Experiencing the Moon is different from just seeing her out there in the sky. We usually take her rather for granted. With the method described below, we can actually discover her for the first time.

The first Meeting

Choose a night when the Moon is as full as possible. You will need a pair of binoculars so you can look at the Moon at close range, examining her clear freshness, and her full, almost sensuous silence. Looking in this way, there comes a realization that the Moon is actually "there" in her fullness and roundness and presence. It is a completely different experience from the flat picture that you usually see. Now you can actually experience the Moon being there in space, inhabiting the space around the Earth.

Allow this perception to enhance your sense of the presence of the Earth on which you are standing, as well. See that the Earth and the Moon are both inhabiting the same space, and allow yourself to feel the subtle magnetism which holds them together. Don't be in a hurry, don't think about the scientific principles behind it, and don't "space out" on the beauty of it. Just allow yourself to feel it, physically, with all your senses.

And now allow your attention to include your own presence, standing there so very small and insignificant, enjoying the wonderful gift of being able to watch and "experience" it all.

The mystery and beauty
of the full Moon brings
all the senses into full
flower.

The Magic of Moonlight

The difference between the Sun and the Moon is that the Sun enables us to see the world around us — this is his magnificent gift. The Moon's gift to us is to light up our inner world, and therefore to illuminate that love which springs from inside us all.

In the moonlight we perceive the reality of the love energy more accurately, the different shades and nuances of emotions, the particular vibrations of other people, and, as we will learn, the different kinds of magic which suit different types of people and the interchanges between them. Moonlight also exalts the scents which are used in the performance of magic.

In the night our senses are more open and receptive, and with the guidance of the Moon they can lead us into the mysteries of love energy more easily. With the help of magic our senses will develop to their fullest potential. And it is with this openness of all the senses that we can truly meet and merge with our partners.

Below: The soft glow of a moonstone helps to get acquainted with the Moon.
Opposite: Astrological clock in Prague, a reminder of a past when magic was more a part of everyday life than it is now.

A Date With Destiny

For many of us living in cities the Moon and her energy can seem very far away. It can be difficult even to get an uncluttered look at a piece of sky, let alone to be able to contemplate the Moon in her soft splendor. But this does not mean that we cannot discover the magic of love in our lives.

The fact is that when we are ready for the Moon — and for her magic — she will find us wherever we are.

However, if we wish to meet her halfway, the following is the best way to do it:

From a lunar calendar (a calendar or a diary which shows the phases of the Moon, her times of rising and setting, and the astrological signs through which she moves) find out when the next full Moon appears in the sign of your natal Moon.

Your natal Moon is the sign the Moon occupied at the moment of your birth. If you don't know it already, this information can be obtained through consulting an Ephemeris or by asking an astrologer.

If your natal Moon is in Capricorn, for example, you will wait until the next full Moon in Capricorn. On this particular night your responses to the Moon are heightened and you will be much more receptive to her rays.

The Moon is not necessarily full in each sign every year. So, it might happen that for one year she will never be quite full in your natal Moon sign. If that is the case then choose the nearest approximation, which should be about two days before or after the full Moon in a neighboring sign. As the Moon changes signs every two to three days it is very likely that you will have an "almost full" Moon in your natal sign without having to wait a very long time.

While you wait, you can practice the Basic Love Ritual, and experiment with the Love Magic practices found elsewhere in the book. When your night comes you will be all the more ready for your lunar rendezvous.

A full Moon, a sandy beach, and a sparkling sea — one of the most potent combinations for magic!

Meeting Your Lunar Ally

If you can manage it, it is best to arrange to be in a place in nature which you particularly like — the seaside, a mountain, a riverbank, a meadow. But if this is not possible, then you can sit outside on a terrace or balcony, or, failing all that, in front of an open window where the Moon can shine in.

If the sky is overcast and you cannot see the Moon at all you will have to wait for the next full Moon in the sign — a pity! But if the clouds allow you to see even a fleeting glimpse of Moon it is perfectly all right to proceed.

Cover yourself up if you need to, and make yourself comfortable. Sit facing the Moon, and breathe gently, feeling as if with each in-breath you are breathing in the soft light of the Moon. With each out-breath, let the cares and worries and thoughts of the day be washed away.

After you have come to a certain calm and stillness inside, close your eyes and ask the Moon to send you an image of the "Lunar You." Who are you, really, in the soft light of the Moon? Not your daytime self, your "Sun

If you are open to her, the Moon can tell you secrets
about your real self, and the lover that would be
best for you.

self" which relates to others, but your "Moon self," which knows secrets, believes in magic, and remembers the innocence of love?

Just try to stay open and receptive, without any ideas about what the answer should be. Allow the Moon to help you, allow an image to arise inside.

When I asked the Moon that question in one of my first encounters I was really surprised. I saw a person walking speedily up a mountain, alone. Like many of us I knew something of my solar self, but nothing of my lunar self. I knew myself as easygoing and company-loving. The Moon was showing me someone who liked to be alone, who liked challenges (climbing a mountain) who liked spartan, almost bare surroundings, who liked hard work.

My Moon is, in fact, in the sign of Capricorn and it is well represented in the above description.

Since that day I have discovered, little by little, how right the Moon was with her image, and that image has been my inner guide, my ally in the world of magic.

After you have thanked the Moon for that image, you can, if you want to, ask her for the image of the lover which would be best for you. Trust the Moon, she has more sense than your fantasies. This second image could surprise you even more than the first one!

It is a good idea to write down the image or images in your notebook after you have received them. If there are some things about an image you don't understand right now, this is fine. If you go back and look again at what you have written from time to time, you will find that your understanding has grown.

There is no need to do anything, just accept the wisdom of the Moon. By getting acquainted with her you are entering the realm of Love Magic.

for Love Magicians Only

Magical implements are best used only for magical purposes. Silver is particularly recommended because it attracts the Moon's rays and multiplies their power.

The Magic Tools

We will now gather together all the objects we will need in this course of magic learning. All these objects will become very special to you. Some of them may be in your possession already, and already very dear to you.

"Caring" is the greatest Love Magic there is. Through constant, gentle caring even the most humble garment becomes charged with the greatest positive energy. You may have experienced this, for example, when putting on a sweater that someone close to you has knitted for you with love. If you are aware, you can sense a subtle change in your mood, in your thoughts, as soon as you cover yourself with the sweater.

In the same way, the implements of magic must be handled with the greatest care. They must be put away in a special place, and if possible must be touched only by you and your loved one.

The most important thing about your magic tools is not their cost or their origins, but that they hold a special meaning and beauty for you.

This is what you will need:

To represent the elements in the Magic Circle of Love described on page 111:

A silver chalice, an essence burner, a silver hand mirror, a silver bowl.

Velvet cloths in the colors of red, green, yellow and blue, to be used in wrapping and storing these implements. Plain cotton pouches of an appropriate size for each.

For the preparation of the Love Philtres described on page 153:

A silver teapot, a silver spoon and a silver tea-strainer. Two copper pots — one to be used only for the preparation of herbs, and one for the preparation of flowers.

A silver or crystal flask or bottle, small enough to be worn around the neck if indicated, by a length of fine but strong silver thread.

Other objects:

A lunar calendar or diary.

A special pen and a notebook to be used only for recording dreams and images given to you by the Moon.

A mat, tapestry or carpet large enough to draw the Magic Circle (about two meters square).

Candles of various colors including white, red, green, yellow and blue, and at least four silver candleholders.

A box of matches to keep with the candles, and a big box in which to store candles, holders and matches.

A deck of tarot cards, wrapped in a velvet cloth of a color of your choice.

A silver or crystal flower vase.

Fine paper such as parchment, on which to write incantations and spells.

A silver box in which to keep the written spells.

Many of these objects are suggested, when possible, to be made of silver, because silver is the metal consecrated to the Moon. This metal attracts the Moon's rays and multiplies her power. When doing Love Magic with silver implements the strength of your incantations is multiplied.

If silver should prove too difficult to obtain then choose crystal, or glass, or porcelain.

Gold is not a good choice — it is the metal consecrated to the Sun, and Love Magic, as we know is a Moon magic.

Do not worry too much, though, if your implements are not well matched, or if they are not quite as beautiful as you would like them to be. Be patient, and use the best of what you have and can find. In time you will see that as your magical powers grow you are able to attract those objects which you need.

Moon-bathing the Magical Implements

This is a very good practice to use for all your magical implements. It is a practice which you can apply, as you wish, to whatever object you like — for example a photo of your beloved or a present which you wish to be specially "charged."

Wait for the next full Moon night. If it happens to be a full Moon in the sign of your natal Moon it is so much the better: it might be worth waiting a month or two for that.

Place the objects you wish to charge in front of an open window facing the Moon.

The Love Magician's world is full of vibrant color, from
fruits and flowers to magical stones and herbs.

One hour's exposure, when the Moon is very visible and at its fullest, is enough — especially if weather conditions make it impossible to leave the window open for a very long time!

Light a candle of your favorite color, and leave it burning for the duration of the Moon bath. This means of course that you need to remain awake and watchful, in order to re-light the candle if it should burn out, or be blown out by a gust of wind.

This is very important. If you should fall asleep and let the candle go out before you have put away your objects, it would be wise to do the ritual again at the next full Moon.

Your awareness, your attentiveness, is of the utmost importance for all magic, and this is symbolized by the burning candle. When you allow your attention to wander during a ritual, not only does your magic surely not succeed, but you can also get into some kind of unexpected mess by confusing words, gestures, or implements.

We can use the example of driving a car. In normal life we generally use our powers at a low level, which can be compared with driving very slowly down a country lane. In this case, falling asleep at the wheel could, at the most, mean a bump on the head. But while practicing magic we are calling on our powers at a very high level, and an accident here is more like an accident on a highway, going full speed.

So be careful and watchful of your actions, move slowly, and always remember what you are doing.

The Magic of Colors

Another wonderful tool, easy to use, to see and to find, is color. This is a tool which you can use freely in the preparation of your space for magic.

Color abounds in nature: we can combine the magic properties of flowers, stones and fruits with those of color so that their power

Learning the effects of different colors and how to use them can help us to bring new joy and love into life, both for ourselves and for our lovers.

becomes more focused... We can surround ourselves with a certain color and consciously let this color help us to bring about the changes wc wish to make in our love and our life.

Magic uses all the senses in the choice of appropriate colors, because what we perceive with the eyes is only a part of the quality a color has. In fact with training, colors can be perceived even with the eyes closed, just by touching or by inner "sensing."

In our practice, there are four basic colors, each associated with one of the four Elements used in Love Magic: red belongs to the element of Fire, yellow to the element Air, blue to Water, and green for Earth.

Additionally, magic makes use of black and white. Black is the absence of color, white the sum of all colors. Black and white, when mixed with the other colors, give us all the in-between shades which make life so interesting.

A very important color in Love Magic is pink, the combination of red and white. Red is passion and white is purity, so pink gives us the shade for the love of the heart — passionate and giving, sensuous and innocent.

COLOR	RED	PINK	YELLOW
FOOD	Cherries Strawberries Watermelons	Peaches	Bananas Pineapple
PLANT AND FLOWER	Rose Snapdragon Amaryllis	Rose and many other flowers	Daffodils
STONE	Ruby Jasper	Agate Quartz	Topaz
PROPERTIES	Energizing Revitalizing Warming	Softening Loving	Cheering Uplifting Clarifying Dispels confusio
MAGICAL USE	Sex and passion magic A rekindling or new lease on the life of a love affair	Romance magic Beginning of a love Tenderness magic	Quarrels magic Loss and despai magic

WHITE	BLACK	BLUE	GREEN
...e inside of many fruits, such as apples, pears	Blackberries	Blueberries Some prunes	All green vegetables
Lily Hawthorn	Only some special roses are black, some tulips, and some orchids	Forget-me-not	Leaves of most flowers
Pearl Moonstone	Tektite Onyx	Sapphire Turquoise	Emerald
Purifying Elevating	Deep transformation Ending	Brings peace to an emotional situation Relaxing Cooling	Healing for the body Harmonizing the body's energy
...ure Love" magic	Banishing magic Putting an old, past love to rest	Love-emotions magic Jealousy magic End of a love affair	Enhancing love and appreciation for the body. Lovemaking magic when combined with red.

This love altar brings together the protection of the self-contained wisdom of the East, and the soft luster of the woman's inner secret, symbolized by the pearls.

The Love Altar

Creating a Love Altar in your house, or in your garden if you have one, will ensure that a part of yourself is always "in love," no matter what you are doing. Even when you are not actively thinking about it or concerned with it, a part of you will keep the flame of love burning through the altar. And if you make sure that your altar is always cared for, fresh and tidy, you can be sure that your love life will benefit from it tremendously.

So, if there is no lover in your life, and you wish for one to appear, make yourself a Love Altar and you will have opened the road for your lover to find you. If you are already in a relationship and are happy with it, invite your partner to join you in creating your Love Altar together. This altar will be the pulsating heart of your love life, which you can keep flowering and rich by adding new offerings to it.

Singles Love Altar

In a place of your choosing — the best places are the bedroom, a special meditation room, or a garden — set up a little table. On this table you will place your Protector, which is an object such as a small statue which strongly inspires you, and next to it a small flask or bottle containing the essence of a flower.

Some of the flower essences that can be used to invite love into your life are jasmine, which brings luck in love, rose, which inspires romantic love, or sweet violet, which will bring softness and vulnerability into your life. Or, experiment to find any other essence which makes you feel loving and lovable.

If you love the sea, you can add a seashell or even a few pearls to your altar. Pearls, especially, contain a very warm, precious energy. In the world of magic they symbolize the woman's inner secret, and they mean "long-lasting love." In fact they are a classic gift between a man and a woman when the feeling is one of permanency in love.

If you should wish for "everlasting" love a small diamond on your love altar is sure to fulfill your desire. A diamond is not so easy to come by, for sure; but then it is also not so easy to find everlasting love!

What to do if, on the other hand, what you want is just to have a good time, relax and

Put a chili pepper on your love altar to add a little spice to your love life!

enjoy a few warm nights, without the hassle of a commitment? Use garnet, the stone for good sex and fun, and add to the altar a little...red pepper!

Complete your altar with a candle, which you will light at sunset every day, for a few minutes at least, and a fresh flower.

The flower can match the essence, or it can be just any beautiful flower in season. Take care to keep the flower always fresh, changing it when it begins to fade. Whenever a wish has come true, take this flower and hang it upside down to dry in a dark room or in a cupboard. Then place it in the box where you keep your written incantations. This flower is charged with strong magic and can help you in casting spells.

One word of warning: you must remember to keep the flower water limpid and fresh. If the water should become cloudy or start to smell foul, this would be a bad sign. It would mean that you are somehow fooling yourself, pretending to wish for love in your life while in fact you are actively keeping it away.

A snapshot of the two of you together speaks volumes
about the real nature of your relationship.
Choose a beautiful picture for the centerpiece of your
love altar, and help the most beautiful aspects of the love
between you and your partner to flower.

Love Altar for Couples

If you can convince your partner to join you in the making of an altar, this will certainly grant your love more assurance of success than a wedding ceremony itself!

But if your partner is not willing, your energy alone can also work wonders.

Start the altar in the same way, with a little tabletop or

shelf and a small flask of essence to ensure that the "spirit" of love is with you. Instead of the Protector you will place on the altar an image of the two of you together. It can be a beautiful photograph, taken in a moment of happiness and closeness. Or it might be a formal portrait.

For magical purposes it is best to have an image of the two of you together in happiness and love. It will help you focus the energy towards that purpose.

If it really is impossible to obtain an image of the two of you together, you can use two photos, one of yourself and one of your lover, simply placing them next to each other.

Always have two fresh flowers on the altar: red ones for passion, pink ones for romance, white ones for pure love.... And remember, also, a magic stone. They are very strong magic, so use them only if you are really sure of your feelings: a ruby is good if you want a very deep and passionate love affair. Red jasper for a warm, sensuous love. Garnet for sexual pleasure. Diamond for everlasting love. Pearls for a long lasting love. Let your stone lie on a velvet cushion — a dark one for a clear or pale colored stone, a light one for a darker stone.

Lastly, place two candles on the altar which you will light when you are performing magic and, especially, when you are alone with your beloved at night.

One important reminder: nobody but you and your lover should touch or move about the objects on your altar.

PART IV

Creating a Magic
Space for Love

It is important to make your home a place which reflects
the magic of your love.

You are beginning to practice "Love Magic"... You have started to perform the Basic Love Ritual and you have placed a Love Altar somewhere in your house, or in the garden. You can already feel that just doing these simple things is changing the quality of your life. Let this feeling expand. You will look with different eyes at your environment, at your lover, at yourself.

Now is the moment to consider the space where you spend time with yourself, or with your partner, when you are at home. Arranging this space to reflect the magic of your love, or the magic of your togetherness with your partner, is a basic step in helping you to create the right atmosphere for loving.

The bedroom must become a temple of intimacy, the bed an altar of passion. The kitchen should be a sacred nourishment alcove, and the bathroom a magic oasis of purification and relaxation.

This does not mean that you should be forced to remove candles and magic stones in order to get to your toothbrush! It means, rather, that the Magician needs to have around him/herself a space which "vibrates" harmoniously: a space which is free and uncluttered, and at the same time soft and warm and capable of reflecting what s/he wants to express at any time, whether performing the humblest tasks or the most powerful magic.

The Magic Bedroom

Walk into your bedroom as if you are entering it for the first time. The first task in creating a Magic Bedroom is to see that the space is not cluttered. Everything that is of no use to you, either practical or magical, should not stay here.

When two people vibrate in harmony with each other their love-energy fills up the whole space around them, and everything in it becomes alive. Every object, too, releases its own vibrations, and all the "things" and "beings" in the room make a concert together.

If an object is unneeded and uncared for, or maybe even disliked but left where it is just out of neglect, in magic moments it will sound a strident note of unhappiness and spoil the harmony of the concert.

Imagine somebody trying to arouse the

Colors have a strong presence which can help raise the love energy, soothe and relax, or promote cheerful, happy feelings.

magic of love in a room that is full of such things, dusty and stale!

So look carefully at each and every thing in your room: do you like it where it is? Have you become so accustomed to it that for a long time you have not even noticed that it is there? Do you like the object itself, or maybe even love it? Go through each of these things and ask yourself as if you want to keep this object. If the answer is yes, find a special place for it and put it there with awareness and love. If the answer is no, remove the object from the room.

The Color Scheme

Now take a look at the colors in your room. Colors too have a very strong presence. Even white is not as neutral as it might seem. To help raise the love energy a shade of off-white is better. White is a strong, rather hard color, which bounces back strongly anything that hits it.

A subtle shade of yellow will work wonders to promote cheerful, happy feelings. A little blue will help to relax and soothe the most choleric personalities. A strong pink could help those who have trouble being more romantic and playful. Red will bring passion. It can be tiring, though, to be passionate all the time — it is usually better to have red accents rather than a predominance of red. In that way, times of passion can rest against a more peaceful background.

The Bed: Altar in the Temple of Love

If we look at the bedroom as a temple, certainly the bed should serve as its altar. First of all, the bed should be yours. It is fine to occasionally sleep on a friend's bed, or on your parents' bed, but as a permanent place of rest and love the bed should have been slept on only by you and by those invited by you to share the night.

You spend many hours in your bed, probably more than in any other place, and during these hours you are always in full physical contact with this surface. If you have inherited your mattress from someone else you are inheriting a great deal of this person's "vibrations" too. And when you use the bedroom for magic these vibrations will not stay asleep, they will interfere with your magic.

A room where everything is carefully chosen, consciously placed, fully appreciated has a special warmth and vibration of its own.

The same principle applies to couples. Ideally, when two people move in together, they should get themselves a new mattress so they can really start afresh.

But in many cases this is not possible for a number of practical reasons. Let us then, at least, do a cleansing ritual for the bed.

Bed Cleansing Ritual

For this ritual you will need four long-lasting candles, essence of lavender, and a pink quartz, the healing stone. In addition you will want to have ready a piece of parchment, fresh flowers, and a small cloth bag or cushion filled with aromatic herbs.

First place the candles at the four corners of the bed. Burn the lavender essence and then light the candles. Place the stone in the middle of the bed. Under the stone, place a parchment on which these words are written:

Your story past till the candles will last

The candles should burn all night. When the candles have extinguished themselves the bed will be as new, its history gone with the last flicker of the flames.

For the night of the cleansing you will of course sleep elsewhere.

In the morning open wide the windows, find fresh flowers in the fields or garden, or buy them if the season does not permit gathering, and place them around the bed, as shown in the picture on page 57. Place the aromatic herbs upon the bed. The bed will start its new life with lots of beautiful fresh energy and it will certainly grant you many hours of rest, peace, love and passion.

Placement of the Bed

The placement of your bed, ideally, will allow you to look out a window from which the Moon can be seen. For Love Magic the bed should never be placed in a corner, because this will restrict the flow of energy around it making it feel much like a "cage." The best idea is to "tune in" yourself to the energies in your bedroom, and experiment with different positions for its furnishings until you find an arrangement that "feels right."

The important thing is not to be confined by ideas of what is the "right" way to arrange things, and to allow your sensitivity and imagination plenty of freedom in arranging the temple of your bedroom. Finally, the most important factor in placing the bed is to find a position that allows you to see the Moon, to bathe in its light, as much as you can.

Opposite: Four long-lasting candles, lavender essence, and a pink quartz work together to cleanse your bed and transform it into an altar of love.
Below: A morning full of fresh air, fragrant herbs and flowers marks the beginning of a new life for your bed, and for your love, too.

Soft Furnishings

If you are someone who likes warmth and tenderness, soft furnishings will be an essential part of your bedroom decor, to be considered carefully.

Your sheets and bedcovers are as important as the bed, and you should follow the same principles as those outlined for the bed itself. It also helps if they are made of natural, non-synthetic fibers. In choosing sheets and bedcovers, take into account what you have learned about the magical properties of color.

And, as a footnote, I have discovered that lots of cushions scattered on the bed and the floor will help soften the most hardened companion.

Don't forget that any paintings, or images on the wall should also be carefully selected. The best method for selection is to consider carefully each image in turn.

The bathroom is often a neglected, haphazard space.
With a little care it can become an oasis for the body,
mind and soul.

While you are looking, it is good to do the Basic Love Ritual described at the beginning of the book. If you feel helped by the picture you are considering, keep that picture. On the other hand, if you feel that the image somehow evokes feelings that hinder the rising of your inner love energy, remove that image from your bedroom no matter how precious or expensive it is.

The selection process, whether for your paintings and pictures or the objects in your room, is entirely individual. Pink roses might "turn on" one person, and leave another person totally cold. Some people might like realistic images and patterns, while other people feel inspired by more abstract things. The only real guide is your inner feeling.

And if an erotic image is what you like and makes you feel good don't be shy: go for the most beautiful one on the market!!

Because magic is also made of this...be courageous and if you like, outrageous, too. If you have the courage to "put yourself on display" so boldly, not all your guests might like it. But the ones who do are more likely to be partners in the magic that can happen only between people who understand each other!

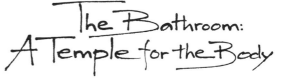

The Bathroom: A Temple for the Body

The importance of the bathroom in a household is often underestimated, and the space allotted to it greatly reduced in favor of other rooms. But for a Magician — especially a Love Magician — the bathroom will be the "body temple" of the house, a place of purification not only for the body, but for the heart and mind too.

Trust your own senses in the beauty products
you use — these are magic tools.

Where better to go after a long day at work to let all the tensions wash away, drop all pretenses and roles, forget all daily worries and find yourself new, fresh, and ready for magic!

The Magician should invest as much care in preparing the bathroom, as s/he does in the bedroom, the living room, the kitchen. And if s/he has the good fortune to have a big bathtub, there is no better place for some of the hottest Love Rituals! Still, even if all you have is a tiny shower room with sink and toilet, there is a lot you can do to help transform this overlooked "utility room" into an inspiring, magical place.

First of all, as you did in the bedroom, make sure that you keep the essential and let go of the rest. Remember that your bathroom can be a temple of beauty, of purification: just as the body is the temple for your soul, so is this water-room the temple for your body. Go through your things and throw out useless bits and pieces of old cosmetics and toiletries which you haven't used for years. Get rid of the dirty clothes hanging on the back of the door, and the toothbrush of the ex-lover who moved out three months ago. And so on...

Keep only the things you really need and that you feel good about. Consider, for example, if you are a woman, the creams which you normally use as part of your daily beauty routine. Do you really like the products you use? Do you like the way they look, the way they smell, the way they feel on your skin and body?

Trust entirely your own senses in this, not the price tag, the name brand, or the advice of others. Beauty products are to be used as magic tools, for it is in that way that they will really work for you. And as with any magic tool, you need to tune in with each product and see if it really helps you feel and look good. No matter how excellent the product, it

Make sure you keep only the cosmetics and toiletries you
really enjoy using, and watch in the mirror as your
beauty grows and grows!

can work well on one person and not on another. The important thing is that you really enjoy the feel and the smell and the effects of the products you use. It might be just a very simple homemade lettuce wash for your face: the thought and feeling of the fresh green lettuce leaves are a delight for you. You can be sure that your skin knows that, and responds accordingly!

The Beauty Altar

As you have a Love Altar, so it is a joy to have a Beauty Altar in the bathroom. It can be just a small shelf or cabinet top.

On your altar you can place the cosmetics and toiletries that you use daily in taking care of your body. Next to these, place a small statue or sculpture that represents the body to you. It can be old or modern, realistic or abstract. The important thing is that the body is naked and that you like the way it is portrayed. It will represent all your positive thoughts and feelings towards your own body and it will carry this energy and release it in the room also when you are not there, so that as soon as you step into the room and see your "body protector" you will feel better.

Keep a candle on the altar, and always one fresh flower.

Just as you did in the bedroom, consider the colors in your bathroom. It is a good investment in your magic to make sure that all your towels, mats and curtains are part of a definite color scheme.

For all healing and beauty magic green and blue are the best colors. But remember a touch of red if you would like to bring your passion to the water also!

In the past people worshipped deities; now they worship lesser gods like prestige and money. My recommendation is that you worship your own body, at least when you step into your bathroom.

The Love Magician's midnight preparations take place in the kitchen. Copper pots are needed for boiling herbs and processing flowers.

The Magician's Kitchen

It would take a whole book to talk about the magic in the kitchen, and the magic of foods.

Here I will give only a few recommendations, because in the practice of Love Magic you will use the kitchen for the preparation of philtres.

Lighting

The kitchen is used for magical preparations usually during the night hours. You will need more light than just candles can provide, but electric lighting will be too harsh. I have an

Herbs, beautiful pots and utensils, and a thorough
scrubbing with natural cleansers all help to grace
your kitchen with the special power needed for
brewing love potions.

of course not in the hot summer! The
presence of the fire element is
most important in a kitchen,
where it radiates feelings of
warmth and nourish-
ment towards the
whole house.

Cleansing and Protecting

Before performing
any magic you must,
of course, clean the
room really well. Use
lemon and sugar on
your brass, vinegar on
all washable surfaces like
the table and counter tops.
And for the floor, add two drops of
lavender essence to the water of the last rinse.

oil lamp for this purpose, the same kind as
my grandmother used to have. The light is
strong enough, yet at the same time warm
and "alive."

If you are lucky enough to have a fireplace
in your kitchen (nowadays we find them only
in rural areas) keep it lit during the magic —

Have fresh herbs on display in a place
where they can "participate" in the preparations and add their own share of power to the
magic. Leave garlic and onions fully in view,
as their strong energy is the best protection
against negative influences.

PART V

Preparation and Purification for Magic Practice

Love Magic starts with the body, and the body loves
being pampered. Listen to what the body tries to tell you,
whether it wants a good scrub with a loofah in the
shower or a luxurious soak in a scented bath.

Being prepared for a Love Magic ritual means above all being relaxed and at ease, and it means to remove, where possible, all obstacles to the flow of the inner love spring.

You have seen in the section on preparing your house how much can be done with the environment to further your own experience of love and magic. Already, having done this much (or even just a small part of it), you will be able to feel that as you step into one of your special rooms you begin to function on a different level. You become more aware of your surroundings and less preoccupied with worrisome thoughts. Your breathing deepens and relaxes, and maybe your emotions are more apparent to you.

If you come into one of these rooms with a partner you will find yourself responding less mechanically to her or him, and be more conscious of the interplay between you.

So much of the important preparation work is done when, having looked at your environment through the eyes of magic, you have then rearranged it accordingly.

Getting in Tune with the Body

Now, just before starting the self-preparation ritual, feel your body. If your work involves sitting all day, or performing repetitive tasks, it is likely that you will feel heavy and a bit sluggish: you can stretch, or take a walk outside (if you live outside town, or in a quiet area), or put on some music and dance to it. Do whatever it takes to make the energy in your body feel fluid once again.

If, on the contrary, you have spent the whole day darting from one appointment to the other, from one job to the next, and you still feel that you are running like a train, relax for a while before doing anything else. But make sure that this relaxation is positive and rejuvenating. Just sitting down in front of the television, although it is very tempting after a full day at work, will not make you ready for magic.

The cleansing and purification rituals of Love Magic are
the surest way to let go of all the strains and stresses
of everyday life and prepare for a world of relaxation
and delight.

Cleansing Ritual for Body, Mind and Spirit

Now have a bath (better if you have created a
magic bathroom) using the light of a candle of
your favorite color while you bathe. Dissolve
a few drops of cedar wood essential oil in the
bath water.

As you lie in the water, imagine that it is
washing away all the thoughts and emotions
that you have gathered in the day. Remind
yourself, if you need to, that even the most
troublesome situations always pass eventually, and often sooner if we don't nourish
them with the energy of our worry and anxiety.

Lie back, close your eyes, and feel the rise
and fall of the water's warmth on your skin as
you breathe in and out. With every in-breath,
feel that the fresh scent of the cedar is entering to cleanse you. And when you breathe
out, let your breath take all your tensions and
thoughts away.

After you have relaxed and rejuvenated
your body, mind and spirit, you are ready for
the next step.

Special robes for magic should be made of natural fibers,
and solid colors are best.

Magic Coats of Many Colors

The clothes you wear for Love Magic don't have to be in any way strange or different, but personally, I prefer to keep a set aside and to use them only for that purpose. It is best if they are comfortable, of course, and of a natural fiber such as cotton, linen, wool, or silk.

I like to wear a kimono style robe, and I have a few in different

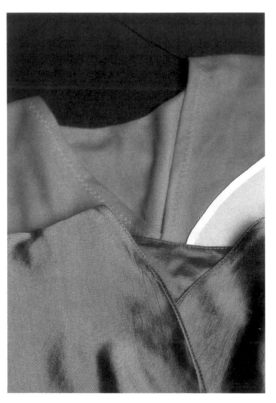

colors so that I can choose according to my mood at the moment. If I feel my energy is low and needs a pick-up, I will wear the yellow or the pink one. For the times when I feel a little "off," not well in my body or spirit, I have one in an emerald green: just wearing it starts a healing process within me. If I am anxious, tense, worried, I wear a blue one.

It is for you to experiment and see what styles and colors make you feel beautiful, awake and, yes, magic!

Caring for Your Magic Robes

Remember to care properly for the clothes you use for magic. Wash them by hand (your own, or your beloved's), and dry them in the shade. They should not absorb too much of the sun's strong energy, but if it is possible, it is good to dry them outside so the fresh wind can disperse any negative charge that might have accumulated on them.

Finally, when they are not in use, fold them (don't hang them up) and put them away in the same place where you keep your other magical implements.

It's a good idea to keep your magical implements together in a special trunk or box, so you always know where they are when you need them.

A Time and Place for Everything

At this point, some readers may be feeling that this is all too much, when life is already so full, with children, work and a husband to deal with!

But it is really just a matter of organizing yourself — I should know, with two children of my own and plenty of work to do! Here are a few hints I have learned from experience, to help you "keep it together."

Keep all your magic paraphernalia in a closed box. I have an old wooden chest which belonged to my grandmother. Lock it with a key and you will never find your little girl playing dress-up with your magic gown!

For the two hours or so in which you practice magic, make arrangements for your privacy (and that of your partner if you are doing it together) to be undisturbed. Love Magic happens with the light of the Moon, so most often at that time the children are asleep and the telephone quiet. But if there is any doubt it is far better to disconnect the phone and arrange a caretaker for the children. Your space and privacy in these two hours are of enormous importance.

Wash your gowns after the magic, and hang them to dry right away. It takes just a few minutes and by the morning you can fold them and put them away. Your symbols and implements should be stored immediately after the magic.

With a little planning and care, and just two hours a week taken from a late evening or an early morning you can have a rich and fulfilling magic life, which will take nothing away from your normal routine.

PART VI

The Magic Circle of Love

Love Magic can bring a new love to your life, or new life
to your love. And the Magic Circle can show you
the path to the new way of relating that is exactly right
for you.

Drawing the Magic Circle of Love is the ritual which will bring all our preparations to fruition. Before we begin with the creation of the Magic Circle, however, it is important to understand the significance of each of its components. Once we are grounded in this understanding, the power of magic is ours, and all our magical implements are our allies. If we should fail to understand, and try to use the Magic Circle in order to fulfill the desires that arise out of our misunderstanding, we will find ourselves in trouble, without fail.

Not that our wishes will not come true — often they will, just to remind us to be careful of what we wish for! And if we refuse to learn the lesson, then Magic will slowly withdraw her hand from ours, and leave us on our own until some time in the future when we are more receptive to the gifts she has to offer.

Magic Sex Magic Relating

Most of us are all too familiar with the pitfalls of ordinary love affairs. We come together with another and it is beautiful in the begin-ning — love always gives us the opportunity to see through the innocent eyes of magic, every time it comes freshly into our lives. But our habits are old and our prejudices are strong, and magic is always new, and fragile as a rose.

In matters of sex, our old habits and preju-dices depend very much on our upbringing. Many of us have been taught to think of sex as shameful, especially outside of marriage. And this message is given to us most strongly at the time when our sexual energies are just awakening, when we are in our early teens. So even if we somehow manage to "outgrow" the attitudes that have been enforced upon us, we often carry their shadows into our adulthood, and even into our marriages! We enter sex reluctantly, furtively, fearful of being hurt, or somehow punished for our "sin."

For men, especially, the harm done by these repressive attitudes is made more com-plicated by the famous "double standard." It is all right for men to have sex before mar-riage — "boys will be boys," after all. But it becomes a competition, a subject of secret whispers in the gymnasium. To have sex

A pure sharing of innocent delight, with no shame, no conquest to be made, no goal to reach.

means to have made a "conquest" and has very little, if anything, to do with loving.

So it is that we have created the classic situation where a woman cannot reach orgasm (how can she enjoy something that is shameful?) and the man reaches orgasm in two minutes, rolls over, and starts snoring!

With the help of Love Magic, we can throw the Moon's soft light on the shadows that haunt our attitudes towards sex, and begin to heal ourselves. Then lovemaking becomes a pure sharing of innocent delight in the body — no shame, no conquest to be made, no goal to be reached. We can reach peaks of ecstasy together, or we can just cuddle and fall asleep, it doesn't matter. Because we have learned to love and respect our own body and its energies, we can also love and respect the body and energies of our partner. With this love and respect, most of the time we sing in harmony. But if sometimes the song is a little flat, so what? Tomorrow is another day...

The Four Elements of Love

The love energy which you can feel rising within yourself during the "Basic Love Ritual" is focused and made concrete in your life through the vehicles of the four elements. These four elements are always present, in different degrees, in the world of love and relating.

The study of the four elements is essential in Love Magic as it is in all other magic. In this section we will look at the elements and

The four elements of Water, Fire, Earth and Air,
recognized since ancient times as the special ingredients
that, along with love, "make the world go 'round!"

their meanings for us in our love relationships. We will also look at the symbols used to represent each of the four elements, and the Love Magic methods that are used in connection with them.

Air

Color: YELLOW
Symbol: THE MIRROR
Magic methods: VISUALIZING, DREAMING

In Love Magic the element Air is related to the platonic aspect of love, the quality of love that comes from accepting and understanding the other person. This love is the love between friends, which can exist on its own, or as part of a relationship between lovers.

The element Air represents the intellect, thinking, understanding and communicating. When it is undeveloped, or immature, it can manifest itself in a tendency to argue, to judge or blame others, to imagine problems and difficulties that don't exist.

As we grow in our own self-understanding, however, this element develops into the ability to take a distance from our own problems and desires — and, in doing so, have a greater possibility of seeing things from another person's point of view. By and by, as "understanding" deepens, we come to recognize the same fears, the same needs, the same joys in everyone. They might take different forms in different people, but they are, in essence, the same.

This is the precious gift of the element Air. At its highest potential it can bring an all-encompassing vision which knows that all people are as one. And if "all people" is a bit too "airy" for you, certainly you will at least be able to see in yourself and your lover the "oneness" which brings true love and compassion.

When the element of Air is undeveloped or lacking in a relationship it will be very difficult for two lovers ever to be at peace with each other. They will not have the ability to take a distance from their own problems and to consider the needs and feelings of the other. They will have a constant tendency to "blame" each other for whatever tensions exist in their relationship. This kind of relationship can be very passionate, with dramatic fights and exciting sex. But it will lack staying power, as the two partners sooner or later

Air — when it's not polluted! — helps us communicate clearly, without the need to fight or blame. With Air as an ally in Love Magic our words grow wings to fly into the skies above.

become exhausted by the continuous state of war they are living in.

Method for developing Air

If a couple, or a person living alone, wishes to develop and "grow" their Air qualities to a higher level, the first step is to disidentify with all the thoughts and words that make up their arguments, judgments and blaming.

One method I have used, which can be great fun, is called "gibberish." Just babble and shout nonsense syllables, allowing your body to move and shake off the sounds. It is a very good method for "getting out of your head" when you find yourself chewing over a problem or a grievance without reaching anywhere. And it is the most effective argument-stopper ever, provided your partner is not so angry that s/he could be dangerous! When one of you bursts into gibberish, how can either of you do anything but laugh?

The sensuous, physical aspect of love, represented by
the element Earth, is one of the most important factors
in our happiness.

If you do gibberish alone, try to go on for at least five minutes — the longer the better, up to an hour is a real deep-cleaning! — and then sit for an equal amount of time with your eyes closed, enjoying the sudden silence. If you do it with your partner, agree beforehand that you will sit in silence for this amount of time before you start talking again.

The Air Symbol

The symbol which will represent the Air element in the Magic Circle is the mirror.

It should be a hand mirror, so that it can be easily handled; preferably old, and if it is antique that would be the best. And, again, made of silver.

The mirror, in addition to being an ancient magic tool, symbolizes the reflecting nature of human relationships. We see ourselves reflected in the other, and the other sees him or herself reflected in us. The mirror is a reminder of this aspect of our "human nature."

The Air symbol is placed at the eastern point on the circumference of the Magic Circle.

When it is not being used, the mirror is wrapped in a piece of yellow velvet cloth, and then placed in a pouch made of a thick, plain cotton.

Color: GREEN
Symbol: FRUIT BOWL
Magic method: MASSAGING, WEARING

In Love Magic the element Earth represents the sensuous, physical aspect of love. It is the love of the body — but that does not necessarily mean only a sexual relationship. For example, the love of a mother for her child can be very sensuous, as they both enjoy touching, cuddling and physical closeness.

In our western society it is not usual for friends to be close physically, and this is especially true for men. Hugging and kissing are reserved for lovers, and for a few special occasions where it is socially acceptable for people to be exuberant and demonstrative. These are usually the kinds of occasions where there is quite a bit of drink going around as well, like weddings and similar kinds of celebrations.

Nevertheless, sensuousness is one of the most important factors in our happiness, and

To make friends with the Earth, the feet are a good place
to start. Because it is there that we contact the "mother"
that sustains us, supports us, and gives us life.

it is a sad reality that denies so much of the physical intimacy which we should be able to enjoy. We see the results of this repressive atmosphere in pornography and other forms of sexual perversion. Our natural, spontaneous sensuality is distorted and twisted, like a tree that has had its roots cut, or has not had the freedom to grow into the sky.

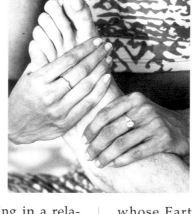

If the Earth element is lacking in a relationship, the couple will be quite hard put to sustain a joyful, fulfilling partnership. They will most often stay together only because of their need for security — which tends to be a big issue for people whose Earth is undeveloped — or out of a sense of "duty," or "for the sake of the children." But the home they provide is too often lacking an atmosphere of real warmth and caring.

Method for Developing Earth

This is one of the most painful elements to have lacking in one's life, especially if the lack has been caused by a trauma. If this is the

case, you need to be very gentle with yourself or your partner in healing it.

In couples, it is most often one of the partners whose Earth is most undeveloped. The other, feeling physically rejected and not understanding the causes, then withdraws into him/herself and the problem just grows worse. If this is the situation, then the partner whose Earth is most developed can be a tremendous help to the other, and find him/herself growing upwards in the Earth element in the process.

Whatever the case, whether you are working with your partner or yourself, the first step is to make a connection with the Earth. And the best place to begin making that connection is with the feet.

Massage each foot in turn, taking plenty of time to go gently and firmly into the tissues and tendons, and remembering to also pay attention to each of the toes. A foot massage is a beautiful way to show your love for your partner, and a beautiful way to thank your

Green is the color that belongs especially to Earth, and helps to heal all wounds connected with the sensuality of the body.

own feet for connecting you with the Earth every day. As an extra luxury, you can soak the feet in warm water, and dry them with a soft, fluffy towel, before you do the massage.

During the day, whenever you think of it, become aware of your feet on the ground. If  you are standing still, see if there is any tension in your feet and let them relax. If you are walking, notice the way your feet carry you. And, notice how this "noticing" affects the rest of your body.

Finally, pay attention to your shoes. Are they comfortable? Do you take care of them, and like the way they look? If the answer is no, treat yourself to some new ones. You can start with a new pair of house slippers, if nothing else.

Soon, you will see, your feet will begin to enjoy their new sensuality so much that they will spread the good news to the rest of your body, in a rising of delight very much like your practice of the Basic Love Ritual.

The calming effect of Water can be found in many places in nature. It represents both the depth of our emotions and the support that enables us to float on top of the sea of emotions when we relax.

The Earth Symbol

In the Magic Circle of Love the element of Earth will be represented by a silver bowl with some beautiful seasonal fruit in it. Preferably apples, which are the love fruit par excellence. Apples are also available the year round.

In winter, dried fruits and nuts are also good for Love Magic. In summer there are many beautifully scented and colored fruits to choose from. Follow your own taste and feelings in this: it is your own magic!

The fruit you buy to be used in performing magic should be kept separate from ordinary fruit. And ideally it should be organically grown, or at least pesticide-free. When you bring it home, wash it carefully and dry it with a special cloth. You can keep it on your Love Altar until it is time to use it for magic, and of course you will use fresh fruit for each ritual.

Fruit is Earth's most precious gift to man. It is so freely given, and so easily received by our bodies. It nourishes, it heals, it is pleasant to all the senses: it is beautiful to look at, good to touch, lovely to smell, delicious to eat.

What comes closer to a description of a wonderfully sensuous lover?

The bowl which contains the fruit is made of silver, and should be about 20cm in diameter. After the ritual it is wrapped in a piece of green velvet cloth, and then replaced in its plain cloth pouch.

Color: BLUE
Symbol: A SILVER CUP FILLED WITH WINE
Magic method: DRINKING, BATHING

The love of the heart, of the emotions, is represented by the element of Water. This is the romantic love with which poems and stories are filled. It is the love that brings tears and laughter and all the emotions in between. In magic, this love-expression carries a lot of strength, so it must be handled with care.

It is easy, especially for women, to bring an excess of Water into their love affairs. (This is in large part due to women's education and upbringing, and it is changing slowly). If their Water nature is immature, they will use "emotional blackmail" on their partners to get what they think they want, making the man

The element Water represents the romantic love with
which poems and stories are filled.

feel guilty with outbursts of
tears. Or they might withhold
sex and warmth as a way of
taking revenge for some
wrong that they think their
partner has done.

Of course for men the re-
verse is often true — the Water
element is not one they feel
comfortable with, and they
have difficulty expressing their
emotions. To compensate for
their own lack of maturity in the Water element, they often choose one of the other elements — this is reflected in "types" such as
the "Don Juan" (Fire), the "bring home the
bacon" type (Earth), or the man whose constant message is, "I need my freedom" (Air).

When it is developed to its highest potential, the Water element brings a quality of
sweetness into our lives, even in the midst of
pain. A person who "knows how to swim" in
the water will be comfortable with his or her
emotions, but not in danger of drowning in
them. S/he can laugh or cry with ease, and
enjoy the release and the freedom it brings.
S/he knows that emotions are as ephemeral

— and as refreshing — as a
passing breeze, so s/he does not
try to hang on to them when
they are happy nor hold them
as a grudge when they are sad.

Method for Developing Water

The next time you are feeling
some strong emotion, and it is
possible for you to do so, find
a big cushion, go into a room
where you will not be disturbed or disturb
others, and let yourself express all your feelings to the cushion. You can beat on it if you
feel angry, cry into it if you feel sad, curse it if
you feel jealous or hurt. Let yourself really
"go crazy" with your emotions, until you
exhaust yourself with the effort. The cushion
will not mind, and you can always apologize
to it later.

When you are completely exhausted, lie
down on your back, close your eyes, and feel
what is happening in your body. Come back
to yourself, to the life energy that is flowing
within you. If a thought comes — "I'm so
angry" — try changing it. Change it to "anger

A right balance of Water can help us to appreciate both happiness and sadness, solitude and togetherness, pleasure and pain, knowing always that "this too will pass."

is happening" or "there is a feeling of heat in the belly." This is disidentification, and disidentification is what allows us to enjoy our ride on the waves of emotion.

You can also do this exercise outside in nature, if you have the opportunity. The trees and the earth and the sky are very accepting, and full of the magic of love.

The Water Symbol

In our Magic Circle the element of Water is represented by a silver cup filled with red wine. The wine must be filled fresh at each sitting, of course, and it should be poured into the cup from a flask used solely for this purpose. The older and the better the quality of the wine, the better it is for magic purposes.

Of all libations, wine is the most magical, as Bacchus knew hundreds of years ago. Wine is used in the rituals of many different religions, from the holiest to the wildest. A little wine helps us to relax, allow-

Can there ever be too much Fire? Well...yes, when a love
affair is so intense that it hurts.

ing the love energy to flow more freely in our body-soul. Particularly, wine strengthens the heart and gives power to the spring of love energy inside.

The silver cup will be emptied and polished after the ritual, wrapped in a piece of blue velvet cloth and then replaced in a plain cotton pouch.

Fire

Color: RED
Symbol: A SCENT BURNER
Magic method: INHALING, BURNING

We come now to the element Fire. What would love be without Fire? A cool exchange of gifts between casual acquaintances. A simple coming together and parting without pain and without ecstasy.

Fire is the element which carries the senses into sensuousness, the mind into flights of imagination and vision, the emotions into a passion for living life in all its many dimensions. Fire is the transforming energy which gives life and vitality to all the other elements, bringing them to new levels of intensity.

I am almost tempted to say that there can never be too much Fire. But that is wrong, of course; a flame too high is likely to burn you. When a love affair is so intense that it hurts...it is good to take some distance and, at least sometimes, divert your attention to other matters. Chances are you will need the diversion soon, anyway, because this lack of maturity in the Fire element most often means that the "love affair" is really a "lust affair" and will pass as soon as the territory gets too familiar to be any longer exciting!

At its highest manifestation, though, Fire is the element that gives real longevity to our relationships. It is the element that most helps us to see each day as completely new, and each meeting with a lover as a first-time meeting with an exciting new stranger. For in fact we are strangers, every time we meet. We are changing every day, moment to moment, and the fire that burns to ashes all in its path is a beautiful reminder of that fact. With the right balance of Fire in our lives, we are burning the past before it can become a dull, boring routine. And as we burn the past, we are free to create the present, fresh and new and innocent, as if we have just been born.

As we burn the past we are free to create the present,
fresh and new and innocent, as if we had just been born.

Method for Developing Fire

Set up a safe place where you can have a small fire — even a warming candle inside a large tin on your balcony will do. The idea is that you should be able to burn small pieces of paper without causing a hazard to anybody or any thing. The time to do this is at night, just before preparing yourself for bed.

A good way to start is with the fears and worries that you know you always tend to have: "I feel awkward when I meet people for the first time," or "I get so jealous when I see my lover having fun with somebody else." Write them down, as briefly and accurately as you can. Next, read them aloud and then burn them in the fire. Watch attentively as the paper turns brown, the writing begins to disappear, and as the flame finally consumes the paper.

Now wait one week, and do this again. See if anything has changed. In between, you can use the same method with any specific problem that arises in your day-to-day life that you would like to burn.

Practice this method for three weeks, and then on the first night of the fourth week, switch your emphasis. Instead of "problems" and worries, write down the things that make you feel most happy and joyful. "I love the scent of fresh flowers," or "It makes me so happy when my lover tells me how good I look." Burn these things too, and clear the way for even greater happiness and joy in your life.

Follow the same procedure as before, burning the things that you feel are "always" true, and using the period of one week in between for the everyday things — "There was a beautiful sunset today." Again, watch to see what changes.

At the end of the six weeks, you will find yourself waking up each morning as if for the first time, feeling fresh and innocent and new. This is an especially good exercise for couples to do together, to settle old quarrels or to commemorate a particularly exquisite night of togetherness. Imagine burning a piece of paper containing the words, "This was the highest we have ever gone together in making love"... and gaining the promise of the Fire element that you will surely go even higher!

The gift of Fire to man: it intensifies our experiences to the point where all the impurities are burned away, and only a fragrance remains. That fragrance is the fragrance of ultimate love.

The Fire Symbol

In the Magic Circle of Love, the element of Fire will be represented by a scent-burner. Scents are an integral part of the love of the heart and of the flesh. Among the oldest memories we have from childhood are those of scents: how our mother smelled, our bed, our house. Scent is one of the vital qualities which can attract us inexorably towards a person, or turn us off completely.

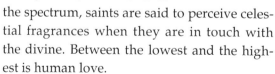

Scent also forms a bridge between the animal and the divine: animals know when their mates are in heat by smell; at the other end of the spectrum, saints are said to perceive celestial fragrances when they are in touch with the divine. Between the lowest and the highest is human love.

This is the gift of Fire to man: it intensifies our experiences to the point where all the impurities are burned away and only a fragrance remains. That fragrance is the fragrance of the ultimate love.

Tarot cards have been used for centuries to reveal the
patterns and opportunities that shape our lives.

Love Tarot

Most readers will already be familiar with the
tarot cards, a deck of cards specially designed
and used to answer the queries of the soul.
The figures portrayed in them are archetypes
representing the steps each human being
encounters during his voyage on Earth
towards happiness and fulfillment. Tarot
cards are almost as ancient as man, and there
are now on the market hundreds of different
kinds.

For Love Magic I have used the Rider-
Waite deck, which is very popular and easy
to find. The deck contains 78 cards, of which
56 are called the "minor arcana" and 22 the
"major arcana." For Love Magic we will use
only the major arcana.

If you have never used tarot cards, it is a
good idea to spend some time learning about
them first. There are several good books
explaining the tarot, which are usually available
for purchase in the same place as the cards.
But in addition to this reading, it is important
to spend some time looking attentively at each
card and considering what it means to you.

The tarot cards are used in the Magic
Circle of Love to help you to clarify the issues
you are concerned with, and thereby
strengthen the magic that you perform. They
can be especially helpful when you are not
quite clear about what is troubling you.

For example, you might have some appre-
hension about your lover. He or she seems
withdrawn, or maybe even cold towards you
recently. But you are not sure...maybe it is
only your imagination, and you have often
been accused of being over-sensitive.

It is hard even for you to define what
magic you would like to perform. Is it just
that you would like your lover to love you
more? Or is the issue really that you would
like to be able to ask your lover about this situation, you are reluctant because you fear
that it might just be your imagination?

In such a case, choosing a tarot card while
you are sitting in the Magic Circle will help
you clarify your situation, and to define the
kind of magic that will benefit you most.

Let us say, using this example, that you
have drawn the card, "The Moon." This card
tells you that there is a misunderstanding or
deception in your situation. You were right to

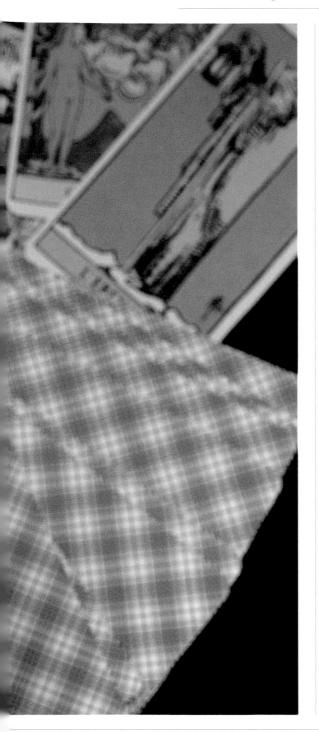

The guidance of the cards, together with your own intuition, can help you see reality more clearly.

feel that something was amiss, and with this guidance from the cards, and help from the magic that will be indicated by the Magic Circle, you can approach your lover and clear up the shadows.

To help you in interpreting the cards, the chart on page 100 shows the usual meanings for each of the 22 major arcana of the tarot. The meanings given must be understood only as indications: when your feeling about a particular card is different you should follow your own intuition. And of course if you have already been using the tarot, you will continue to use the meanings you are already familiar with.

The Fool

Now is the moment to take a risk in matters of love. Dare yourself! Try something you have never done before, take a step without worrying about the consequences.

The Magician

Start something new, on your own. It can be a study or a hobby or a new job or interest. Your life will be greatly enriched by this now.
For a woman in particular: if there is a new man in your life, he is the right one for you. Trust him, and trust yourself with him; what you can do together is truly magical.

The High Priestess

Trust your intuition entirely. If you have any doubts in a love matter, you must first of all clarify what your own feelings are. The answer lies within you.
For a man in particular: the woman in your life can help you understand whatever your problem is. Talk with her and trust her.

The Empress

Nurturing is the key to this situation — warmth, care, attention, good food, and lots of cuddles. Be open to this aspect of love — magic can help you. For a man in particular: there is a strong womanly figure in your life. This woman loves you!

The Emperor

This card represents security, stability, confidence, and trust in your own power. In Love Magic, it is not the moment to do something risky, but to build on what you already have. If you are a woman, there is a man in your life right now, or will be very soon, who is very serious about you.

The Hierophant

Better not try to figure it all out by yourself. Ask the advice of a wise person: it could be a friend, but more specifically an advisor, a doctor, a therapist. Sometimes this card can mean that an existing relationship is going to be legalized by marriage.

The Lovers

This is a time for sharing. Whatsoever your question is, it cannot be solved by you alone. You will benefit from the insights of your partner, or some other person whom you love deeply. Let her, or him, know your inner thoughts and feelings.

The Chariot

You need to take yourself into your own hands, and not let outside considerations or momentary whims determine what you do right now. Ask yourself, without any prejudices, if you are doing what you really want to do. If yes, stay with it, without worrying about others. If not, change direction. You have the strength and power to make what you want of your life.

Strength

You need not force anything. Relaxing into what is happening to you will make everything clear.

The Hermit

It is a time for aloneness. Your present dilemma is your responsibility, and no one else's. Take some space from your partner, or from the social activities you have been engaged in, and find time to be alone. Search for the answers inside yourself.

Wheel of Fortune

There is, or will be soon, a major change in your love life. It can be a change in the environment, or in your routine. The change will sweep off the old cobwebs and bring a new shine to life.

Justice

You need to act out of sound judgment in this matter, and out of a sense of fairness. Put aside passion and let your wisdom bring you the clarity you need to deal with the situation.

Temperance

Be patient with your beloved and with yourself. You will not gain anything now by forcing things, or by trying to be in control. Take things as they come, and the situation will work itself out as it should.

The Hanged Man

The situation you are in now, or one you are about to face soon, will stretch your limits! But even though it might feel uncomfortable, it is expanding your capacity to love. When old restrictions begin to dissolve, it can cause pain. But soon they will let go and be healed, and you will know that whatever you have gone through was worth it!

The Devil

Accept your sexual urges and instincts. This is the moment to free yourself, to be playful, and just enjoy your body and yourself.

Death

It is time to let something die. It could be a relationship, an old way of relating to yourself, old ideas about love, or old ways of relating to a partner.

The Tower

An unexpected event in your love life shakes your very foundations. This change is unavoidable.

The Star

Keep your heart open to hope for the best possible love to happen in your life — with your partner if you have one, or with someone new. It is a fertile moment, don't look back. Make yourself beautiful and ready to receive the gift.

The Moon

There is deception or misunderstanding in or around you. It could be that your lover is deceiving you, or that you are deceiving yourself. Or it could be that are misreading signals from your own heart or your partner's. It is time to find a way to bring light into the shadows, so that you can see clearly what is real and what is just a dream.

The Sun

Express yourself, and all the love that is in your heart. Bring yourself into the light. This can be the card of a new love entering your life, the beginning of a new relationship.

Judgment

It is a time when you are reminded of a truth that you had forgotten, or a time when you can no longer ignore a truth that you had suspected but not wanted to acknowledge. People, or feelings, which you thought were buried, are coming back to life. There can be great joy or great sorrow in this card, but whatever the case, it is a necessary step in your love life.

The World

All happiness and success in love is within you to achieve now. Recognize yourself in your freedom and beauty, for you have all you could ever want.

For Love Magic we bring together all our tools... to create a circle which can be an immediate doorway from the mundane world of everyday affairs to the mysterious and wonderful world of magic.

Drawing the Magic Circle

Drawing the Magic Circle is an age-old practice; our prehistoric ancestors would light a fire and huddle around it, forming a circle with their bodies. Keeping out the dark, the cold, their fears, while inside the circle the hypnotic presence of the flame would join the group into a single feeling of warmth and light.

Since then, wise men and women, witches and magicians of all times have been casting circles: to keep outside the darkness of ignorance, and to focus inside the light of truth and magic.

For Love Magic we bring together all our tools, the tarot cards, the elements, the colors, in order to create a circle which can be an immediate doorway from the mundane world of everyday affairs to the mysterious and wonderful world of magic.

"Drawing the Circle" is the preliminary ritual to all practices of Love Magic. It is the moment when you focus on the matter at hand, and ask Love to speak to you, to clarify any questions you may have (the tarot cards help in this), and to point out a magic course of action through the Four Elements of Air, Water, Earth and Fire.

When

The circle is drawn at night, under the soft eye of the Moon. To choose the appropriate night and time consult your lunar calendar. The Moon must be visible, and in the sign she was at your birth. That means if your natal Moon is in Pisces, you must wait until the next time the Moon transits the Pisces constellation. At the most, you will have to wait three weeks for the right night.

To set the time, again consulting your calendar, you will see when the Moon rises and sets, and when she is in fact visible. For example, say the Moon enters Pisces at 0:47am on the 25th. She rises at 8:26 am and sets at 20:10pm A good time to do the ritual would be in the early evening, after the Sun has set and the Moon is still quite visible.

Where and How

For the Magic Circle of Love the bedroom is

Following pages: Steps in creating the Magic Circle of Love. Once the cards and all the symbols are in place, sit where you can see the Moon. If you can't see her, then sit facing the direction where you know the Moon to be.

the best place. All you need is an uncluttered area of floor at least two by two meters. But the living room or a study will do fine, provided that you can ensure privacy and quiet. The most important thing, as you will see, is that you can see the Moon from the space where you create your Magic Circle.

Lay down a carpet or a mat of the required dimensions; this you will keep only for this purpose, and it should not be used for anything else. When you are finished with magic, you will roll it up again and put it away.

Using a white string or a ribbon as you would a compass, mark the four cardinal points of your circle: east, west, north and south.

At each of these points you will place candles, not to be lit until you actually begin the ritual.

Unless it is a full Moon night, clear of clouds, it will be impossible to see well enough to perform the ritual by the moonlight alone. And the four candles of the circle will probably be insufficient to provide good lighting. So you can light as many candles as you wish, and place them everywhere in the room. Besides giving you plenty of illumina-

tion they will create a beautiful and warm atmosphere.

Each of the four points of the Magic Circle represents an element, and now you are ready to place the symbols of the four elements for love. The south is the place of Fire, the north, the Earth. West is the place of Water and east the place of Air.

Each of the four symbols of the elements is placed next to the candle holding its place: a silver mirror for the element Air, a silver bowl with a seasonal fruit in it for the element Earth, a scent burner for the element Fire (if possible, burn myrrh or frankincense on this occasion), and a silver cup containing wine for the element Water.

Once you have placed the candles and the symbols of the elements, take the 22 major arcana of the tarot deck, and sit in the circle facing the Moon. Of course, the best possible situation is one where, through an open window or balcony, you can see her. But if this is not possible it will be sufficient to acknowledge the position of the Moon and to sit facing towards her.

Now take the tarot cards and shuffle them three times. Cut the stack of cards three times

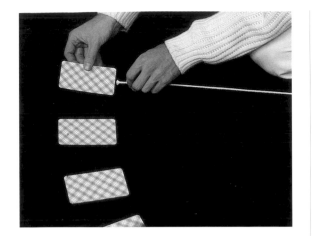

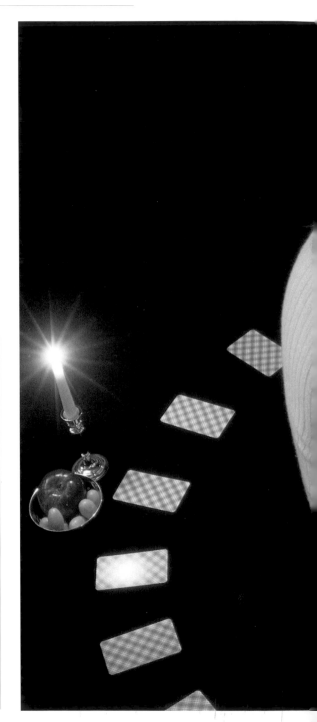

It is important that you keep your focus on the question
at hand, not letting side issues come in and
confuse you.... And wait to see which one of the
elements "calls" you.

with your left hand, and lay out the cards in a circle as shown in the picture on page 106. The four candles representing the four cardinal points, and the symbols of the elements, will stay on the outer part of the circle.

Once the Magic Circle has been drawn in this way, it is time to prepare and dress yourself as indicated on page 68. Take the phone off the hook, unplug radios and TV systems, close the door: you are now ready to begin.

The Ritual

From outside the circle, beginning with the place of the Fire element and moving in a clockwise direction, light each of the four candles representing the four points of the compass. Use the matches you have put aside especially for this occasion.

Now step into the circle with your left foot forward, and sit inside it, facing in the direction of the Moon. Acknowledge her by closing your eyes and visualizing the silver disk of her beautiful presence. Of course if you have the possibility of looking at the Moon through a window or balcony from where you are sitting inside the circle it is so much the better. In this case, you will be looking at

her without closing your eyes. Imagine her light entering into your heart, dispelling all the shadows there. Feel the magnetic pull of the Moon on your own inner love energy. Just by allowing yourself to be touched by her you can feel the inner love spring waking and gently flowing upwards.

When you feel you are attuned with the Moon and her energy, it is time to acknowledge the presence of the Four Elements. Turn towards each of them, beginning with Fire, as you say the ritual words:

Under the soft light of Moon,
I see you FIRE,
who give life to my love.
Under the soft light of Moon,
I see you WATER, who give
nourishment to my heart.
Under the soft light of Moon,
I see you EARTH,
who give body to my passion.
Under the soft light of Moon,
I see you AIR, who give
wings to my compassion.

Page 111: Quick guide when placing the magic tools on
the Magic Circle.

Then come to rest at the center once again, facing the Moon, and focus on the question at hand. You need to be very clear during this part of the ritual, and must not let side issues come in and confuse you: If the issue troubling you at this time is jealousy, keep your heart and mind on it, even though it might be painful. If other thoughts come in — how you met the first time, your friend's new lover — don't follow them. Let them pass, or push them aside (gently!) and go back to your chosen issue.

It is very important to stay focused if you want magic to work in that particular area of your life.

Say, aloud, one short sentence which defines your problem. It can be very brief and simple. For example:

"I want help with my jealous feelings towards Mark."

"I am starting a new love affair, and I want to know how it will be."

Your question can be specific to a particular situation, as in the above examples, or it can be a more general question, but in this case it must always be concerned directly with you:

"What do I need to look at in my relationship with Mark right now?" — not, "How does Mark feel about me?" Or,

"What can I do to allow more love into my life?" — not, "I want other people to love me."

After you have asked your question, again come to rest in yourself, your mind quite empty, your eyes closed, and let one of the elements "call" you.

You will feel it perhaps in your body. That's how it is for my husband. He says: "It is the element behind me that calls!" (or the one on his right, or left).

Or you might "see it" in your mind's eye. Or you might "feel it" with your heart (it is so for me). Whichever way it works for you, you will know it, without any doubt.

Once the element has answered you, turn towards that element and choose one card from the portion of the circle that lies in front of you. Let your hand be pulled towards the card, much in the same way you have allowed the element to "call" you (page 113).

Turn the card over, and, if you need to, look up the meaning of that card.

You now know which of the four elements

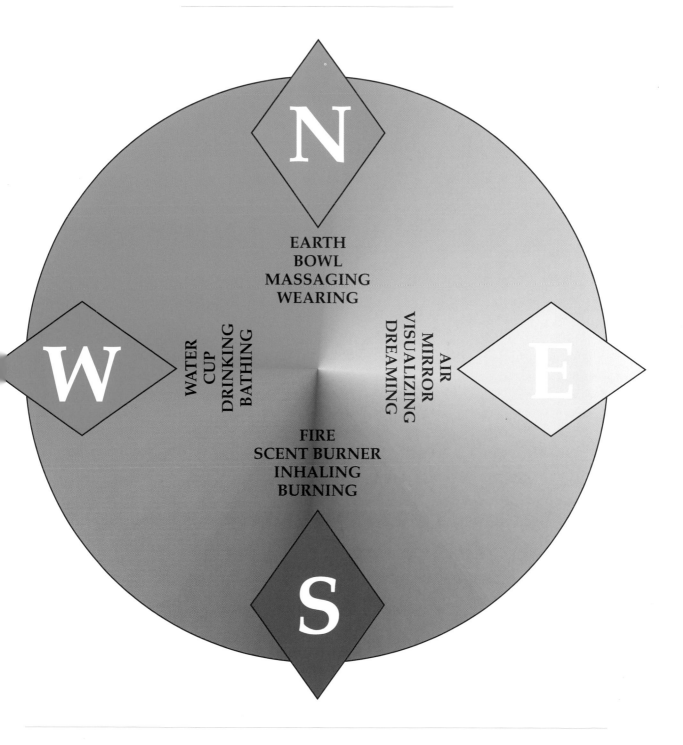

N

EARTH
BOWL
MASSAGING
WEARING

AIR
MIRROR
VISUALIZING
DREAMING

E

WATER
CUP
DRINKING
BATHING

W

FIRE
SCENT BURNER
INHALING
BURNING

S

Choose your tarot card from the portion of the circle that is in front of you after you have been "called" by one of the four elements.

will benefit your magic (and therefore the method to use), and you have the indications given by the card. You are ready to choose the appropriate magic to perform (page 140 and 208), to be able to set the night and time for it, and gather what you will need to accomplish it.

This is the end of the Magic Circle ritual. Step out of the circle first, and then extinguish the four candles by pinching them, walking around the circle in an anti-clockwise direction.

Sharing the Circle of Love

If you are in love with someone there is nothing more natural than wanting to involve that person in Love Magic. After all, that is the beauty of love, to share, and it is the beauty of Love Magic also. Performing magic rituals with your beloved next to you makes them so much more powerful, and also more fun.

The essential thing when you do magic in a couple is that you are both willing to be as honest as you know how to be. Honesty is the first requirement; without honesty it is use-

less to start. It is more important than being in love, more important than having a lot of strong sexual feelings towards each other, more important than being able to communicate well. It is even more important than actually "liking" each other!

Above all, you have to know that you will have the courage to admit to the truth of what is happening to you, moment by moment — admitting it both to yourself and to your partner when you need to. And you have to know that your partner will have the same courage, the same commitment...to truth.

How to know if your partner feels this way? You can, of course, ask him or her. But basically, the rule to go by is this: do you have any doubts inside yourself? Because if that is the case, whether your doubts are wrong or right, you should not enter into magic with that partner.

This does not imply a moral judgment of any kind: it is not to say that people who can be honest are "better" in some way. There are many reasons why people find it hard to communicate openly, and this is a quality that can grow and develop over time. But for magic, it is just a practical consideration.

Choose your partner for
the Magic Circle of Love
with care!
The most important
qualities are honesty, a
willingness to be
vulnerable, and a
commitment not to judge
or condemn the other.

When you practice magic with a lover, you need to be assured that both of you will be able to expose yourselves and be vulnerable, without risking the judgment or condemnation of the other.

When you move in the realms of magic, where the borders between the tangible and the intangible become thin, you cannot afford to worry about the truthfulness of your partner's responses. This is the first rule.

Otherwise it is up to you: choose someone you feel good with, of course. And remember that the stronger the energy between the two partners, the stronger will be the magic. If you are "mad" about each other, or even if you are very "mad at" each other, this energy has a terrific potential to be used in any magic practice. And, when it is used in the right way, it can yield terrific results.

Instructions for Couples

In the Love Circle ritual only one of the partners will bring forward the issue and turn a card. This person will be called the "active" partner. The other person, the "passive" partner, is present to give strength and focus to the first one.

Practicing magic together can bring magic to many other
aspects of a couple's life too!

If, for example, a couple comes with the issue of "poor communication" between them, they will come to a decision together about who will be the active and who the passive partner. They need not make a communication issue out of it, though! Just tossing a coin to decide is fine.

Once they are inside the circle, they will both focus on the issue at hand, but when the moment comes the active partner will speak out the sentence which defines the issue, will "listen" to the elements and will turn the card.

You can prepare yourselves together or individually, this does not matter. Create the circle together: one person can place the candles and the symbols, the other can lay the cards.

The woman is the one who should step first into the circle, the man second. If the lovers are two men, or two women, they should decide beforehand who goes first into the circle.

Getting in Tune

When both partners are inside the circle, before anything else they must let their hearts, bodies, and minds fall in tune with each other. The following is a well-known tantric practice which is ideally suited to achieving this attunement:

Sit facing each other, and breathe gently in and out, focusing the attention on the breathing of the partner. At this stage you are not trying to change your own breathing rhythm: you are just breathing gently at whatever pace comes naturally to you, at the same time being aware of the partner's breathing.

The second stage: when you feel relatively peaceful and calm, and you feel that your attention is now settled in this room with your partner, gradually let your breathing fall in tune. Soon you will see that when your partner breathes in, you breathe in. When s/he breathes out, you breathe out.

Don't force it...nothing terrible happens if you miss one beat. This practice brings you in tune with each other, and settles your attention on what you are doing.

When you have reached an attunement, acknowledge this to each other without using words. Then say the words of greetings to the four elements together, and proceed through the ritual as explained above.

PART VII

I Put a Spell on You!

It is best not to perform any magic at all on the night
of the black Moon — except some very, very special cases
when you want to end something, once and for ever.

Now that you have completed the ritual of the Magic Circle of Love, you are ready to perform the magic of casting spells. You have already the guidance of the Magic Circle in choosing what kinds of potions and incantations you will use, and in what way. In addition, you will need to know the magic associated with the essences and love philtres which make up the Nine Magical Keys, and how to determine the right timing for the magic you want to perform. These tools are given to you in the following pages.

But the most important tool of all is your own intuition and feeling. Follow your heart, and your magic cannot go wrong!

Magic Timing

It is the Moon that will guide you in choosing the right timing for your magic. For this you must keep in mind three essential aspects which influence the magic: the lunar phases, visibility and the astrological signs through which the Moon transits.

The Lunar Phases

From the nights in which we see only one tiny sliver of Moon shining in the sky, to the nights of the full Moon and back again to a sliver, the Moon is passing through what are known as lunar "phases." The first quarter and second quarter are called "waxing" Moon, followed by the full Moon, and then the third and fourth quarters, called "waning" Moon. Finally, there is the black Moon or new Moon.

The Moon-magic chart on page 122 shows the different kinds of Love Magic which belong to the various phases of the Moon.

During the WAXING MOON her influence on magic is one of "expanding." This influence is positive and promotes growth. The waxing Moon is the best time to perform magic related to the beginning of a relationship or of a love feeling, starting something new in your current love life, or to promote coming back together, re-kindling passion and magic for the future.

When the MOON is FULL her energy is very strong, stable, and "enlightening." Much of Love Magic happens under the full Moon.

PHASES	1st to 2nd quarter Waxing Moon	Full Moon	3rd to last quarter Waning Moon	Black Moon
RISING	Noon	Sunset	Midnight	Dawn
SETTING	Midnight	Dawn	Noon	Sunset
VISIBILITY	Late afternoon to late evening	All night	Second half of the night to early morning	Not visible
MAGIC	Increasing a new lover's passion, beauty. Bringing in love feelings	Full power for any man	Banishing jealousy or any other unwanted emotion or situation	End of love

Left: Match the Moon to the magic, and she will
help you every time.
Below: The waning Moon is particularly good for letting
go of a love affair.

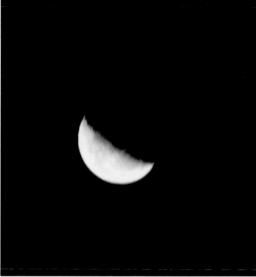

Under her patronage you can perform wedding magic, promote staying together, or find the sources of courage in love. It is an especially good time for all the magic which has to do with true hearing and true seeing, as the light of the Moon in these nights will certainly help you dissolve all shadows.

Also, problems of impotence and frigidity are best dealt with under the full Moon.

During the WANING MOON strong emotions recede and big problems can be put into perspective. It is a good time to deal with jealousy, pain and any other heartache which you want to take a distance from and finally banish from your life. You can let go of a love affair in this time, and also abandon any negative love pattern you might have.

Finally, the night of the BLACK MOON is a night when it is best not to perform any magic at all —except some very, very, special cases when you want to put something to death, once and for ever. On this night no soft light will shine on you. You will be, so to speak, "unprotected." All the same, the banishing forces are very strong in this time. Use this night only if all other courses of action have failed, and you really need to symbolically "kill" something out of your life — a love affair which lingers on in your heart even though you have been separated for years; the memory of some hurt suffered in the past which is contaminating your life now; the unwelcome and maybe even frightening presence of an unwanted suitor.

One thing to remember always is that the magic of the Moon changes slowly through the phases. After a black Moon for example the energy of the Moon moves slowly away from an intense banishing magic towards the growing, expansive phase. So if you want to

Left: The full Moon is particularly good for dealing with problems of impotence and frigidity.
Below: If you are having problems with jealousy, wait for a waning Moon to help you put things in perspective.

promote a new love affair, let a few days pass after the black Moon. The same is true for the full Moon — full Moon magic can be practiced successfully two days before the full Moon and two days after. Of course, the closer you are to the actual full Moon the stronger the magic.

Visibility

Another thing to remember when you schedule your magic is that you must make sure the Moon is actually going to show up for you!

You must know the time of the rising and setting of the Moon, and you need to keep in mind that she will not be visible all along her orbit from rising to setting.

Make sure the Moon is going to be visible during the
time you perform your magic. If heavy clouds obscure
the sky, best to wait for another night.

Generally, the first quarter Moon rises at noon and sets at midnight, but is visible from late afternoon to late evening; full Moon rises at sunset and sets at dawn and is visible all night; last quarter rises at midnight and sets at noon, and is visible the second half of the night and early morning.

For magic the Moon must be visible, so if you are performing magic during the last quarter, you must perform your magic between midnight and five or six in the morning, when the Moon is still visible in the sky.

Sometimes it is possible to see both the Moon and the Sun in the sky. In this case, even though it will restrict the possible times of performing magic, it is better to wait until the Sun has set. The Sun energy is very strong and it can easily overshadow the more subtle and gentle magic of the Moon.

What happens if the sky is overcast and you cannot see the Moon because of the cloud formations? If the clouds are so dense that you cannot see the Moon at all, you must reschedule your practice; but if you can see at least an occasional glimpse of the Moon between the clouds then it is fine to proceed.

Moon Transits

The other important factor to bear in mind when you choose the appropriate timing for your magic is which astrological sign the Moon is transiting.

The Moon highlights and magnifies the energies of the different signs as she transits through them: if you are dealing with issues of emotion, it is good to choose a time when the Moon is transiting through one of the Water signs (Cancer, Sorpio or Pisces); if it is a matter of understanding, then an Air Moon (Gemini, Libra, Aquarius) will do for you; if you are dealing with the intensity, or lack of

Right: If you have a knack for mathematics you can
follow these instructions.
Otherwise, you can always ask an astrologer!
Following pages: A quick guide to the best Moon signs for
different kinds of magic.

it, in a situation or with the essential vitality of something, choose a Fire Moon (Aries, Leo, Sagittarius). Finally, when you are looking at the physical side of things choose an Earth Moon (Taurus, Virgo, Capricorn).

The Moon stays in each sign for two and a half to three days. So, for example, if you wanted to perform magic under the waning Moon, with the Moon in an Air sign, you would look into your lunar diary to see when the Moon next starts to wane, and which astrological signs she will be passing through.

In the example shown on page 129 the Moon is full in Cancer on the 8th of January. As she begins to wane she moves through Leo (Fire), Virgo (Earth) and then into Libra at 9:30 am on the 13th. Libra is an Air sign, so it will be right for your magic. But you will have to wait until the next night, the 14th, because at 9:30 am on the 13th, the Moon will soon be setting. The following night, between mid-

Natal Moon

The Natal Moon is the position the Moon was in at the time of of your birth.

Transit Moon

The Transit Moon is where the Moon will travel the day you want to perform your magic. You can refer to the opposite page for your calculations.

night and the first hours of the morning, will be the right time for you.

Of course you will need a lunar calendar to figure all of this out. I like to use a calendar that comes in diary form, so that I can note on the appropriate pages the magic I want to perform and list all the things I will need for it.

The Natal Moon

Alternatively, you can use the time when the Moon is transiting in the same sign as your natal Moon. This transit will give your own intuition and psychic powers an extra boost. When you "draw the circle," it is this Moon which helps you. You can also use this transit when you are in doubt as to which element would be good for your magic, and therefore you don't know which other transit to use.

The full Moon in your natal sign is of course a very important time, to be dedicated to magic.

The way you calculate the exact position of the Moon (or other planets) in each astrological sign is the same regardless of the type of ephemeris you choose to use. The example on this page shows the position of the Moon at 0hr and at 12hr of each day, Greenwich Mean Time (GMT). Some ephemeris only give the position of the planets at 0hr or at 12hr. You will need to first check your ephemeris to find out which time it is based on.

To get the position of the Moon you need to check the difference between the time you are in and convert to GMT. Most countries adopted summer time a few years ago, so you will also need to make these adjustments. For example if you want to perform your magic in New York at 8:25 pm in January, this corresponds with 15hr 25 GMT.

In an ephemeris the Moon and other planets (symbol) are usually at the top vertically. Horizontally, for each day, you will find the sign (symbol) the planet is in. On its left the degrees and on its right the minutes and seconds.

A small table also shows the phases of the Moon. It indicates the day and time of the phase, the phase (symbol) and the sign it is in (symbol), with on its left the degrees and on its right the minutes.

☽ Phases & Eclipses			
Dy	**Hr Mn**		
1	3:38	☽	10 ♈ 44
8	12:37	○	18 ♋ 15
15	4: 1	☽	25 ♎ 1
22	18:27	●	2 ♒ 46
30	23:20	☽	11 ♉ 6

How to calculate the exact position of the Moon

1. Translate the degrees in minutes (also called minutes) by multiplying the degrees by 60 and adding it to the minutes. Moon on the 13th of January at 0hr: 24° 16′ 36″ = 1456′ (you can ignore the seconds). Moon on that day at 12hr: 1° 29′ 47″ = 89′

2. Calculate how many degrees the Moon travels on that day: 1456′ – 1889′ (when the Moon travels through another sign you need to add 30° — the number of degrees of each sign — and also convert it in minutes: 30° x 60′ = 1800′) = 433′ — the Moon travels 433′ in 12hr (it changes every day).

3. If you want to know where the Moon will be at a certain time:
   a) Calculate how many minutes (degrees) the Moon travels in one minute (time) 433′ divided by 720′ (12hr x 60′) = 0.6′
   b) Multiply this amount by the minutes of time 665′ (11hr 05′ translated in minutes) by 0.6′ = 399′
   c) Reconvert in degrees: 399′ divided by 60 = 30° 39′. Since this number is bigger than 30°, deduct 30° and you know you are in the next sign. So at 11hr 05 the Moon is at 0° 39′ in Libra.

Day	☽		12 hr ☽	
1 F	8 ♈ 55	1	14 ♈ 56	46
2 Sa	21	1 31	27	9 50
3 Su	3 ♉ 22	19	9 ♉ 39	29
4 M	16	1 51	22	29 49
5 Tu	29	3 45	5 ♊ 43	53
6 W	12 ♊ 30	22	19	23 11
7 Th	26	22 12	3 ♋ 27	8
8 F	10 ♋ 37	29	17	52 39
9 Sa	25	11 54	2 ♌ 34	18
10 Su	9 ♌ 58	55	17	24 43
11 M	24	50 38	2 ♍ 15	41
12 Tu	9 ♍ 38	54	16	59 27
13 W	24	16 36	1 ♎ 29	47
14 Th	8 ♎ 38	32	15	42 36
15 F	22	41 49	29	36 8
16 Sa	6 ♏ 25	49	13 ♏ 10	27

4. If you want to know what time the Moon goes into a new sign (Libra in this example):
   a) Calculate how many minutes (time) the Moon takes to travel one minute (degree). 720′ (12hr x 60′) divided by 433′ = 1.663′
   b) Subtract: 1800′ (the number of degrees of each sign, converted in minutes) minus 1456′ (the degree the Moon is at 0hr, converted in minutes) = 344′. This gives you the minutes (degree) during which the Moon travels in Virgo from 0hr to the time it enters Libra.
   c) Since the Moon takes 1.663′ (time) to travel one minute (degree), multiply 344′ by 1.663′ = 572′. Divide by 60 and this gives you the time the Moon enters Libra: 9hr 32′.
      If you get a number above 24hr, this means you subtract 24hr and add one day.

	ARIES		
	LEO		For intensity and vitality
	SAGITTARIUS		For <u>sex</u>

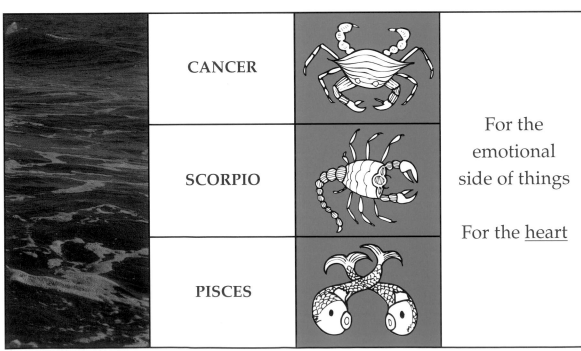

	CANCER		For the emotional side of things
	SCORPIO		
	PISCES		For the <u>heart</u>

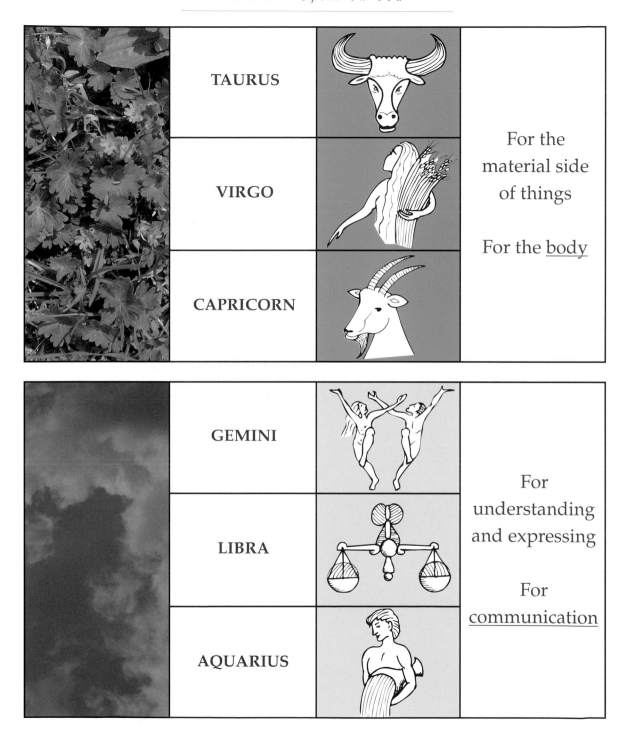

	TAURUS		For the material side of things
	VIRGO		
	CAPRICORN		For the <u>body</u>

	GEMINI		For understanding and expressing
	LIBRA		
	AQUARIUS		For <u>communication</u>

Essential oils and love philtres can add romance to your life in countless ways.

The Nine Magical Keys

From the immense array of magical tools that are available, I have chosen, for Love Magic, five essential oils and four love philtres made from a combination of ingredients. These are known as the Nine Magical Keys.

Essential Oils: Magic Keys for the Inner Lover

The essential oils contain in themselves the very nectar of the magic of the flowers from which they are extracted. Fortunately for Love Magicians, these oils are getting easier to find, as they are more and more used by healers and therapists for a variety of purposes. They can be found nowadays not just in specialized shops, but in many regular pharmacies. I love to use them: they are strong, powerful and yet so subtle and permeating.

One drop of rose essence used in a magic way and the heart is singing... One of jasmine used in the bath with ritual words and the body feels like it has been loved for hours.

The five essential oils take care of the inner side of
relating in love, and help you to prepare for it.
The four love philtres are special recipes to help you in
relating to others.

And what could be more alluring than surrounding yourself and your beloved in a sweet, musky scent?

The magic of the essential oils takes care of the inner side of relating in love.

The first two essential oils act on sensuality and sex. Removing fear and condemnation, they help the sexual energy come alive again and reach unknown peaks of passion and enjoyment. The Magic Key N°1, the Sex Opener, increases the capacity for abandon and pleasure in a sexual encounter; the Magic Key N°2, the Sex Healer, helps to dissolve sexual blocks and hindrances that arise from experiences in the past.

The second two keys act on the heart: the Magic Key N°3, the Heart Opener, opens the door to a wealth of new feelings and love. The Magic Key N°4, the Heart Healer, brings to the surface and cures past pains and wounds of the heart.

The Magic Key N°5, the last of the essential oils, is an invaluable help for feeling happy, centered and relaxed when going to a love meeting. It can be used before a rendezvous, before a date, before any important love appointment.

Love Philtres:
Magic from the Inside Out

The remaining four keys, the Love Philtres, are a distillation of the ancient wisdom of magicians all over the world.

Some of the ingredients are little known, like damiana or fo-ti-tieng. Others, like ginseng, have recently gained popularity in the west.

The rich and fertile magic of the fruit trees — the orange, the apple, the cherry, the walnut — combined with the strong and active magic of the herbs, makes up each of these four intense philtres.

Where the essential oils take care of the inner aspect of love — what actually happens inside you, your sexual and emotional responses — the Love Philtres take care of the interacting side of love: how you appear to others, how you communicate with them.

The first two Love Philtres are keys to better communication, to a magical way of understanding others and of expressing yourself. The second two are the magic keys to better appreciation of one's own sexual identity: they will grant you a stronger foundation

A quick reference guide
to the Nine Magical
Keys, and the gifts of
nature that go into them.

in your own maleness or femaleness,
and open you to new ways of
improving your appearance
and your sense of well-being.

The Love Philtres plus
the oils, used in accordance
with the indications given by the
element which is appropriate for you
(see the Magic Circle), will bring
magical help to most of the issues which
might arise in your love life, or the love lives
of your friends.

But you must remember
that these are just indications, tools which magic
uses in spinning her web.
Anything you want to use
can also become a magic
tool. If you want, you can
make up other Love Philtres,
using ingredients which
appeal to you and that you feel
are "alive" to you; or you can use
a whole range of oils, or you can mix them.
Once you have learned the knack of it, the
world of love can be your very own magic
garden.

ESSENTIAL OILS

MAGIC KEY N° 1
The Sex Opener: Neroli
(*Citrus aurantium*)

MAGIC KEY N° 2
The Sex Healer:
Ylang Ylang
(*Cananga odorata*)

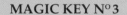

MAGIC KEY N° 3
The Heart Opener: Rose
(*Rosa damascena*)

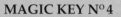

MAGIC KEY N° 4
The Heart Healer:
Jasmine
(*Jasminum officinale,
jasminum grandiflorum*)

MAGIC KEY N° 5
For a Love Meeting:
Melissa
(*Melissa officinalis*)

LOVE PHILTRES

MAGIC KEY N° 6
True Perception:
Orange and Damiana
(*Turnera diffusa,
damiana messicana*)

MAGIC KEY N° 8
Woman's Magic:
Apple, Nutmeg, Vodka and
Fo-ti-tieng
(*Hyfrocotyle asiatica minor L.*)

MAGIC KEY N° 9
Man's Magic:
Ginseng
(*Panax Quinquefolium*)
Nasturtium, Walnut and
Ginger

MAGIC KEY N° 7
True Expression:
Cherry and Heather
(*Calluna vulgaris*)

Each of the Nine Magical Keys can be used according to one of the four elements of Water, Air, Earth and Fire. The methods according to each element are explained in detail on the following pages.

Methods of Magic for the Keys by the Elements

In a moment we will learn the specific uses and methods of preparation for the Nine Magical Keys. But first, let us understand the different methods that are available to us in using them.

You will be performing your magic according to the element which has "called" you during the ritual of the Magic Circle of Love. Each of these elements, as we have seen before, has certain methods associated with it. These methods are described on pages 140 and 141, along with the colors and phases of the Moon associated with them.

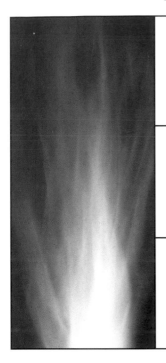

COLOR
Red

MAGIC TOOL
Burner

MOON
Aries
Leo
Sagittarius

METHOD FOR ESSENTIAL OIL

Put two or three drops of the appropriate essence on the essence burner. While burning the essence keep two (or more) red candles lit at either side of the burner.

METHOD FOR LOVE PHILTRE

After drinking the prescribed amount of the philtre, throw the rest into a fire, saying the appropriate words.

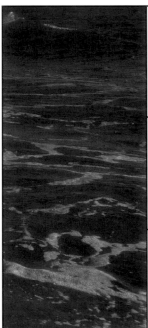

COLOR
Blue

MAGIC TOOL
Cup filled with wine

MOON
Cancer
Scorpio
Pisces

METHOD FOR ESSENTIAL OIL

Put two or more drops of the essential oil in your bathwater. Use only candle light or moonlight during the bath. Observe silence after the bath.

METHOD FOR LOVE PHILTRE

Drink the prescribed sips of the philtre, then throw the rest in living water: the seaside, a river, a pond or a lake.

COLOR
Green

MAGIC TOOL
*Bowl filled with
seasonal fruits*

MOON
*Taurus
Virgo
Capricorn*

METHOD FOR ESSENTIAL OIL

For couples: After preparing yourselves one partner will massage the essential oil, (a few drops mixed with a regular fragrance-free massage oil) into the body of the other. Green candles should be burning for the time of the massage, and silence should be observed.

For singles: If you are alone, choose a part of the body that feels right to you (your feet, your hands, arms, legs, neck or chest, for example) and give yourself a massage with the oil mixed as above, treating your own body as lovingly as you would that of a beloved.

METHOD FOR LOVE PHILTRE

Tie a fine silver string to the flask which contains the appropriate philtre and place it around your neck, to reach the heart or the navel, as indicated by the instructions for the philtre.

COLOR
Yellow

MAGIC TOOL
Mirror

MOON
*Gemini
Libra
Aquarius*

METHOD FOR ESSENTIAL OIL

With the oil, draw a symbol of the eye on your forehead before sleep.

METHOD FOR LOVE PHILTRE

Drink a sip of the appropriate philtre before sleep. Keep the flask under your pillow for the night.

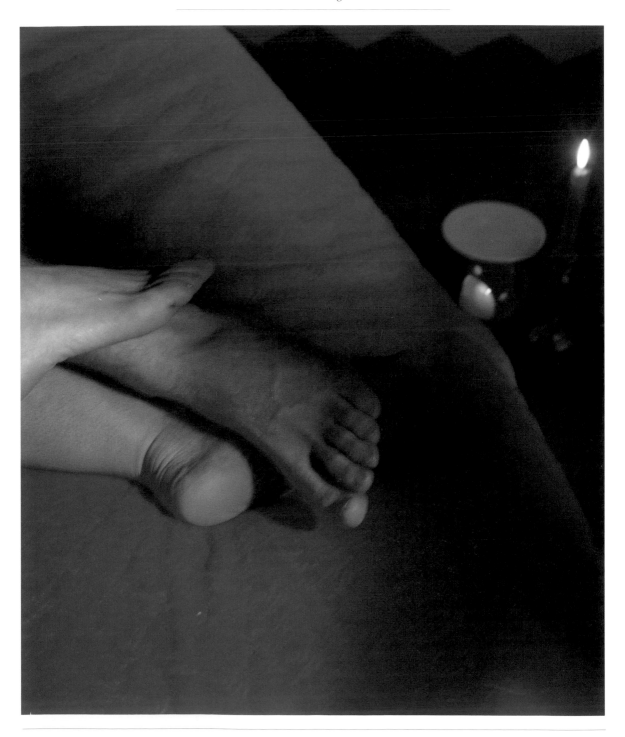

Two or three drops of neroli in a scent burner can help
to make sure that a long-awaited night lives up to
its promise.

Preparation and Magical Properties of the Nine Magical Keys

MAGIC KEY N° 1
The Sex Opener: Neroli
Citrus aurantium

The origin of the name "neroli" is uncertain. It is thought by some to derive from the name of the Emperor Nero, but the most generally accepted theory is that it gets its name from Anne-Marie, Princess of Nerola, who used it to perfume her gloves and her bath water. She was the wife of a famous Italian prince who lived in the sixteenth century; her glove perfume became very popular and gloves scented with it were known as "guanti di Neroli."

The best quality of this essential oil is called "Neroli of Melangola" and is extracted from fresh flowers of bitter orange, or citrus bigaradia. This variety is the best one to use for magic. The other kind, extracted from sweet orange flowers will not have the same powerful effect.

Medicinal Properties

Neroli is highly beneficial for the nervous system. It alleviates anxiety and nervous depression, acting as a natural tranquilizer with hypnotic, sleep inducing qualities. It calms and slows down the mind, and has a striking effect on the heart, diminishing the amplitude of heart muscle contraction. As such it is used in treating palpitations or other types of cardiac spasm. Its action is slow but sure.

Neroli purifies the blood and, if used as part of a massage oil, it improves the circulation.

Magical Properties and Uses

This scent is an invaluable magical help in raising the sexual potential of both men and

Add a couple of drops of ylang-ylang to a scentless shampoo to improve the sheen and condition of your hair. Beware of using too much ylang-ylang, though — it can give you a headache!

women. Its hypnotic, relaxing, expanding magical effect, when used properly, melts away all the layers of tension and anxiety which lead to premature ejaculation in men. Its warming, fear-melting qualities help the woman expand her capacity for excitement and passion in lovemaking. For example...

You have just managed to lure an exciting lover into your magic bedchamber. The night is full of promise: two or three drops of neroli in the scent burner at the foot of your bed will make sure that the promise is kept. Place two red candles at each side of the bed (four in total) and put a red cover on the bed. This will ensure the presence of the Fire element.

Before you do anything else, check the Moon from your window. If she is visible and waxing or even full (the best luck) you can be sure that the night will be memorable, with more good times to come. If the Moon is waning this affair will have a difficult side to it, but still the difficulties are going to be precious because they will force you to let go of some unwanted element in your life. If there is no Moon at all, don't let yourself become too involved: you will have a great time tonight...but the next day you will forget all about it (or he will)!

Neroli magic is also great for those who tend to consume sex too quickly, without fully enjoying the pleasures of it (usually men) and for those who are slow to reach their potential of excitement and passion (usually the woman). In these cases, use neroli in conjunction with the Magic Keys N° 8 or N° 9, "Woman's Magic" or "Man's Magic."

MAGIC KEY N° 2
The Sex Healer: Ylang-Ylang
Cananga odorata

Ylang-ylang means flowers of flowers; it is intensely sweet and smells somewhat like jasmine and almond together. It is originally from the far East: the best kind was formerly produced in the Philippines, but unfortunately that quality is not available anymore. It has a pale yellow color.

Medicinal Properties

The essence was used in the past to combat maladies. It is a fair antiseptic, but more than that it is a tonic for the nervous system and an

It is no accident that the rose is always associated with love and lovers. The rose is one of the most powerful aids to the practice of Love Magic, and can be used in dozens of ways.

aphrodisiac. It is good for oily types of skins, and improves the sheen and condition of hair (add three to four drops to a mild shampoo).

The essence is very intense: used in excess it will give you a headache and nausea.

Magical Properties and Uses

Ylang-ylang, the exotic sweet flower, the strong piercing fragrance, makes your body ripple and your senses reel. Ylang-ylang is the magic sex healer. It will go straight to the heart of the matter and show you where your sexual fears lie, and how they can be healed.

Used with the method of Earth, gently massaging it into the body, this essence will wipe away the fears that violence has left there (see page 204). Used by Fire, letting the essence permeate the room in which you are making love, it will enable you to overcome any fearful moment during sex. Used by Air, it will allow you to know through your dreams what are the causes of your fears (see page 192).

Ylang-ylang is very strong magic and must be used sparingly and with care: never put more than two or three drops in the burner or in the bath water, and when you mix it with oil for massaging do not exceed the amount of three drops per eight ounces of oil.

MAGIC KEY N° 3
The Heart Opener: Rose
Rosa damascena

A love garden without a rose would be unimaginable, and the same is true of practicing Love Magic without the essential oil of rose.

The oil, like the flower, is original to Persia. In fact it was during a love ritual, a wedding, that this flower's essence is said to have been first discovered. It was the wedding of the princess Nour-Djihan and the king Djihanguyr: to embellish the gardens with flowing scented water the king ordered that a

Almond oil is a good base for most essences when they
are used in massage.

canal be dug, and filled with water and rose flowers. It was a very hot summer and the Sun shining continuously on the canals soon warmed up the flowers... before long, an oily substance was seen to be floating on the surface of the water.

That substance was to become the most widely used essence in the world: the essential oil of rose.

The best oil is derived from the roses of Bulgaria, the damask rose. It takes 180 lbs. of flowers to make just one ounce of oil! So of course it is very expensive.

But on the other hand, one little drop is enough to grant you success in love, so you will not need to mobilize all your savings...even though they would be well spent on a successful love life!

The color of the oil is orange-green.

Medicinal Properties

The rose is toning and revitalizing; it soothes the nervous system, aids digestion, and improves the circulation.

As a beauty aid it is used to moisturize, to cool and rejuvenate the skin.

The rose is, of course, a well-known aphrodisiac.

Magical Properties and Uses

As you grow more familiar with this essence you will find more and more new ways of using it, and it will never cease to amaze you. For me it has the unique and wonderful property of facilitating the Basic Love Ritual, the experiencing of rising love energy. I only need to put a drop in the burner and to anoint my forehead with it, and I can feel the joyous fountain bubble up inside me even when I have been feeling stressed, or tired and uninspired.

In my experience, the rose essence is one of the most powerful and versatile aids to performing Love Magic, and you can be sure that it will bring love into your life — in the form of a new lover, if that is what you ask for, or of renewed interest in your old partner. And it will always help you to develop the feeling of being loving and worthy of love.

Jasmine will open the hardest of the hearts to the softness of love and works wonders both on female and male sexuality.

MAGIC KEY Nº 4
The Heart Healer: Jasmine
Jasminum officinale, jasminum grandiflorum

In Arabic "Yasmin", in Persian "Yasumin"...the Chinese called it "mo-li" and in India its name means "moonlight of the grove." This flower has been cultivated down the centuries for its exquisite fragrance and prettiness.

The oil of jasmine is a dark brown, reddish color and has an intense, sweet scent. Like neroli, this oil can be very expensive, especially the French variety.

Medicinal Properties

The oil of jasmine is certainly worth its price tag. Its properties are in fact very strong both on a psychological and physical level. The effect of the oil on the emotional life is uplifting, cheering. It promotes self confidence and happiness, and is good for treating cases of depression and apathy.

On a physical level jasmine works wonders both on female and male sexuality. Mixed with some almond oil and massaged on the body it relaxes and warms, soothing both the mind and the body. Because of the intensity of the scent, it must be used sparingly.

Magical Properties and Uses

Jasmine is one of the most important flowers in a magic love garden, together with the rose flower. It brings the very essence of enchantment and romance. Jasmine will open the hardest of hearts to the softness of love, it will caress the most insensitive skin back to a new sensitivity and pleasure.

When you have bathed using the essence of Jasmine its fragrance will stay with you. This way its action is slow and deep: it might take a few weeks or even one or two lunar months..but the effect will be sure to show itself.

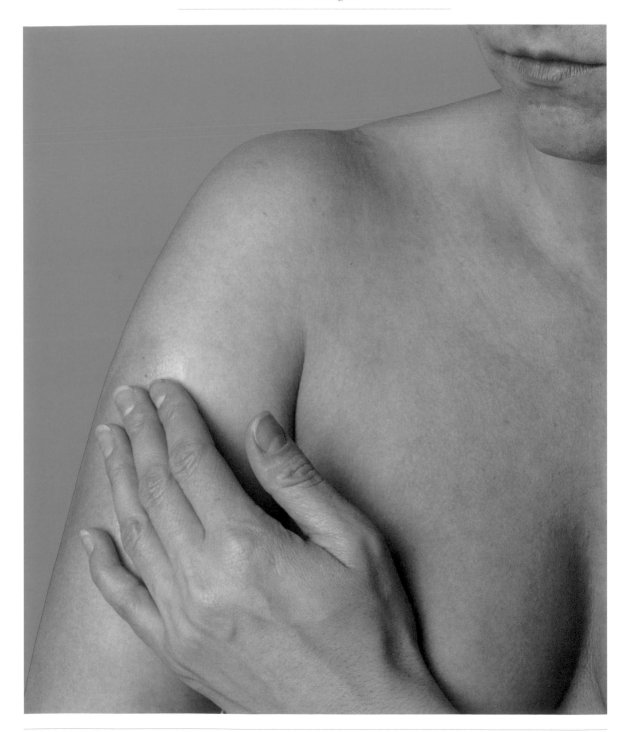

Melissa is truly a good friend when it comes to easing
away anxieties and tensions about meeting that new and
possibly special person in your life.

MAGIC KEY N° 5
Love Meeting: Melissa
Melissa officinalis

This herb, also known as lemon balm, is cultivated throughout Europe, and it grows
wild in fields and forests. It has tiny
flowers, which can be white or yellow,
but the essence itself is taken from the
leaves of the plant. Usually it is gathered
just before it flowers in the early summer.

The scent of this essence is lemony,
but much more subtle and flowery
than that of lemon oil.

The name "Melissa" comes
from the Greek word for bee
— reflecting the fact that the
bees love this plant. Existing records
show that melissa has been used in healing since at least the seventeenth century.

Medicinal Properties

Oil of melissa is an antispasmodic and tonic
of the nervous and cardiac system. It is used
to fight depression, anxiety and also palpitations and sciatic problems. As it releases tensions and contractions in the body, it helps
the emotional system relax into a more joyous
and light state. It also has a relaxing and
soothing effect on the digestive and reproduc-
tive systems.

Massage the whole body with a solution of
two tablespoons full of soya oil with five
drops of melissa added. Or add six
drops of melissa to the bathwater to
soothe away anxiety and nervousness.

Magical Properties and Uses

Don't be misled by the soft, fragile
appearance of the plant. The magic
of the essence of melissa is every
bit as powerful as that of the rose
or of the jasmine.

The essence of melissa is to
be used in magic where there is
a need to soothe your heart, in cases
where the anxiety comes from "nervousness." That is to say, when you are anxious
about a particular event or situation — rather
than the vague and general anxiety that
comes from a deeper or more serious emotional problem.

The water used in brewing the philtres should be pure spring water.

The Love Philtres

For these last four Magical Keys, the Love Philtres, preparation is all important. When you set out to mix the potion check the Moon sign and phase to correspond to those that are suggested for each philtre.

Prepare yourself as you would for a magic ritual: you should be inwardly calm, centered and focused, and outwardly cleansed and dressed for magic (see page 68). The kitchen should also be prepared, as explained on page 62.

Before You Begin...

You will need two copper pots, one for boiling the herbs and one for processing the flowers. You will also need a strainer for separating out the liquid from the herbs and flowers, and a teapot in which to mix the potion. Ideally, both these items should be made of silver. Finally, you need five small flasks made of glass or silver, with corks. The flasks should be small enough to be worn around the neck, on a fine silver thread.

All of these objects should have been pre-

The fruit and flower of the orange have been used for centuries in the love charms and aphrodisiacs of the East, as has damiana (below) in Mexico.

pared beforehand by Moon-bathing, as described on page 36.

The water used in brewing the philtres should be pure spring water, and the philtres should be prepared freshly for each magic ritual you perform.

MAGIC KEY N° 6
True Perception

Ingredients

1. DAMIANA
   (*Turnera diffusa, damiana messicana*).
   This plant, with its yellow flowers and pale green leaves, lives in the desert and is found particularly in Texas and Mexico. Mexican women have been known to drink an infusion of damiana before lovemaking, as an aphrodisiac. But prolonged and excessive use of damiana should be avoided, as it could be damaging to the liver.

For the philtre we use the whole plant. The damiana herb can be found in specialized herbal shops and should be kept in a dark closet, inside a closed glass jar, until it is used.

2. A HANDFUL OF ORANGE BLOSSOMS AND AN ORANGE PEEL.
   The fruit and the flower of the orange tree are a delight for the senses. Orange has been used as a love charm and aphrodisiac in eastern countries for millennia and in the west, orange blossoms are often the centerpiece of bridal bouquets.

Traditionally, the potion is prepared from fresh blossoms, gathered on a full Moon night and prepared in the philtre that same night. If you are in a position to do this, your magic is doubly blessed! But if it is impossible, try to obtain fresh blossoms one night before you perform your magic, bathe them in the light of the Moon the first night, and prepare the philtre the following night.

In either case, if you want to keep some of the flowers for later, gather them while they

When using one of the philtres with the help of the
element Air, the excess liquid must be cast to the winds.

are flowering and steep them in wine for two days and two nights, bathing the concoction in moonlight during the nights. During the entire time the blossoms are steeping in wine, burn a yellow candle next to them. Then, filter the liquid and keep the wine in a dark place until you need it. This wine will serve in place of the flowers in your ritual.

Take the peel of a fresh orange grown under pesticide-free conditions. Traditionally, this should be the first fruit of a new tree. So be sure to choose an orange that feels young and alive to you, and not one which feels like it has been stored in a cooler for weeks.

Procedure

Take two tablespoons of dried powdered damiana to one cup of pure spring water, and boil vigorously in the copper pot for five minutes.

While the herb is boiling, stare intently into the dark water saying these words:

All I will see, all I will know.

You must say the words silently, whispering to yourself, so as not to be heard. The words of a spell are pronounced aloud when you are addressing the powers (of the Moon, of the elements, of an essence), but they are only whispered when they are part of the ingredients to a magic concoction. (That is why witches have always been depicted "mumbling" strange words over their cauldrons!)

After the five minutes have passed, strain the liquid into the teapot.

Next, use the other copper pot to gently simmer a handful of fresh orange blossoms in a half cup of pure spring water — or simply simmer a half cup of the wine concoction, if you have prepared one for this purpose. Add the orange peel as soon as the liquid in the pot begins to simmer. At the same time, murmur these words:

I trust what I see,
I trust what I feel.

After simmering for one minute, strain this liquid into the same teapot, and mix the two liquids together using a silver spoon.

Pour enough in your flask so that it is half filled, then throw away the remainder into the air — off a cliff, into the wind at the seaside, or into the woods or your garden on a

True perception is a philtre which will open your
"magic eyes" and guarantee you the ability to perceive
the truth of your own feelings and those of your partner.

windy day. The idea is that the air should carry off the liquid. If you cannot go out in nature, then cast it out the highest window you can find — checking first to see who or what is underneath, of course! Your philtre is now ready.

The Magic of Key N° 6

True Perception is a philtre which will open your "magic eyes" and guarantee you the ability to perceive the truth of your own feelings and those of your partner. It will also give you trust in what you see and what you feel.

It often happens that love relationships can go through a period where they are plagued with doubt: "Does she really mean it when she says that she wants only me?" or "I feel that he is angry with me, but every time I say so, he denies it. Should I trust myself, or what he says?" These doubts and many more like them are very common occurrences between lovers as people have become further and further estranged from their own inner truth and wisdom — from the core of magic reality that resides in all of us.

This Love Philtre cuts through all the cobwebs of misunderstanding, falseness and pre-

tense, and permits you to have a glimpse of what is really going on. It will also give you the trust to follow this truth, even though it might be difficult.

If used with the support of the element Air, in Dream Magic, the clarity about your situation will come to you at night in the guise of a dream, or of a dream-like image which will make you "understand." That is the method most often used for this philtre. But when the doubts exist at the heart level, when you are not sure of what you "feel," use the philtre in connection with the Water element and there will be no mistaking the direction your heart wants to take you.

MAGIC KEY N°7
True Expression

Ingredients

1. HEATHER (*Calluna vulgaris*)
   This plant flowers in late summer, and covers the fields where it grows in a spectacular carpet of lilac-colored flowers.
   Gather the flowers and dry them by hanging them upside down in a well-aired room.

The soft yet revealing light of the Moon is an essential
ingredient in the preparation of all the Magical Keys.

2. CHERRY BLOSSOM

This delightful pink flower should be used fresh, if possible. If it has to be kept, do it this way:

Take the blossom of the cherry tree when it is in flower, on a full Moon night. Steep the flowers in wine for three hours, under the Moon, and then for three more days in the dark. Then strain the liquid and keep the wine in a flask, well protected from heat and light, until you need it.

Procedure

Take a handful of cherry blossoms and place them in your silver teapot. Pour in one cup of boiling water, prepared in the copper pan used for flowers. Place the teapot somewhere near a window, so that some moonlight can shine on it, and let it stand for ten minutes.

If you like, you can add some cherry liqueur. Pour about a quarter of a cup directly into the teapot, and then expose the mixture to the Moon while you prepare the heather flowers, as below.

Throw a handful of the dry heather flowers into one cup of water, which is boiling in the copper pot used for flowers. Let the pot sit in the moonlight for three minutes, then strain the liquid into the teapot, with the other ingredients. Stir the mixture together with the silver spoon, saying these words — aloud, this time, because of the properties of the philtre:

In the quiet of the Moon,
with the flowers that there bloom
let me say the true words soon.

Now pour some of the liquid from the teapot into the flask, and throw the rest into an open fire — a fireplace, or a bonfire outside. The flames must consume the remaining potion.

Cherry liquor, wine, heather and the fire of life combine
to enable you to express your feelings truthfully and
openly, with compassion and love.

The Magic of Key N° 7

The True Expression philtre enables you to express your feelings truthfully and openly, but at the same time with consideration for the other — with love and compassion.

It is not unusual to find people who will tell any lie just to avoid hurting others or, on the other hand, people who tell the truth about how they think and feel, blurting it all out without any consideration of the pain they might cause. To reach a balance, to be able to be truthful about one's own feelings and experience while at the same time remaining in touch with the partner's responses, is indeed one of the most important arts to learn in love. This Magical Key opens that door effortlessly. It is a door that can change your life forever.

Using this philtre with the support of the Earth, you will need to have it close to your body. Wearing it suspended from a silver thread around your neck, under the clothes, is a good way. After a day or two, you will begin to feel that your whole body wants to express itself. You might choose to change the colors you are wearing, perhaps noticing for the first time how the colors you wear do not really express what you would like to "say."

A friend of mine, who had been using this Magic Key in this way, found that within a few days she was giving away a whole wardrobe of greys and blues and replacing them with pinks and reds: she wanted a new love in her life, and she was finally beginning to express it!

You might also find yourself coming closer to people, touching them. Or you might discover that what you really want is to keep a distance from a situation of physical intimacy that feels false or uncomfortable to you.

Whatever the case, using the True Expression philtre in connection with the element of Earth can bring you more in tune with how your true nature wants to respond to others through the vehicle of your body.

The leaves of fo-ti-tieng, pictured below, have been used in China since ancient times to prolong youth and to enjoy a healthy life. Nutmeg, opposite, has always been considered a "love" spice, used by courtesans to improve their amatory arts.

With the support of the other elements, it will allow you to express your understanding or your emotions. And with Fire, it will enable your whole energy to move in the direction that is right for you, whatever the situation.

MAGIC KEY N° 8
Woman's Magic

Ingredients

1. FO-TI-TIENG: *(Hyfrocotyle asiatica minor L.)* Venus's Navel

This exotic plant, with little violet flowers and flat red fruits, grows in Asia, particularly in China. Since ancient times people in this part of the world have chewed the fresh leaves of fo-ti-tieng to prolong their youth and to enjoy a long, healthy life.

In fact, a well-known Chinese herbalist who used this plant, Li Chung Yun, is famous for having lived for 256 years until his death in 1933! Hence the Chinese translation of the herb's name, "elixir of long life." More recently, a French biologist, Jules Lepine, documented the regenerative effects of this plant on the nervous system and endocrine glands.

Medicinal Properties

Drink a tea prepared from half a teaspoon of ground, dried leaves in a cup of hot water every day, for improved health and a rejuvenating effect. Increasing the dosage to one or two teaspoons a day will have a strengthening effect on your sexual energy.

R.A. Miller, in the book *Aphrodisiacs and Magic Rites*, recommends cooking 120 grams of fo-ti-tieng leaves for six hours, simmering without boiling. This tea should be drunk within three to four days.

Use the ground dry leaves of fo-ti-tieng, which you will find in a specialized herb shop.

2. APPLE BLOSSOMS AND APPLESEEDS

Since Eve gave Adam the apple, this fruit has represented the woman more than any other. If you can manage to gather fresh apple blossoms from a tree on the same night as you are preparing the philtre, that will be best. Otherwise, prepare the flower's wine in

The Woman's Magic Philtre leads to the discovery of the very essence of the woman — her truth, power, beauty and love. Preparing the philtre near a living body of water is best.

the same way as has been described above for the orange and cherry blossoms.

Also, you will be using four seeds from a fresh, "alive" apple. Traditionally these should come from the first apple of a new tree.

3. NUTMEG

This is a spice you are likely to already have in your kitchen. In China it has always been considered a "love" spice, which is brewed into a hot drink given to the courtesans to improve their amatory skills.

4. TWO OUNCES OF GOOD VODKA

Apple blossoms and the combined power of a group
of friends add grace and power to the Woman's
Magic Philtre.

Procedure

For the preparation of this philtre it is best if you can arrange to be near a body of living water: a house near the sea, a lake or a river would be ideal.

This is a woman's magic philtre: it is only for a woman to prepare, and no man should be present in the room at the time of the preparation. If it should happen that a man enters the room by accident, the preparation of the philtre should be interrupted, and rescheduled for another night. The philtre is also only for a woman to drink and use.

In the herb pot bring one cup of spring water to a boil. Add two teaspoons full of dry fo-ti-tieng, and the four appleseeds. Let the mixture boil for four minutes.

Put the apple blossoms into the second copper pot and steep with the vodka. Put the steeping mixture on a windowsill where the Moon can shine on it and let it sit there for nine minutes.

Note: If you are using an apple blossom wine, omit the vodka, pour the wine essence directly into your teapot, and place under the moonlight.

Strain the liquid of the herb and the appleseeds into the teapot, then strain the liqueur of the blossoms into the same teapot. Add a pinch of nutmeg and mix with a silver spoon, saying these words to yourself:

For the woman's magic,
for the woman's love,
for the woman who's true,
like the Moon above.

If you own a real pearl drop it into the brew, and this will increase the power of the potion a dozen times: this is the ingredient of the dark and secret side of womanhood — that side which is unknown even to the women themselves, but which is there, nevertheless. It is the link between the human and the divine that resides, like the pearl in its shell, in the depth of the sea, ensconced in the depth of the woman's womb.

If there are other women with you as you

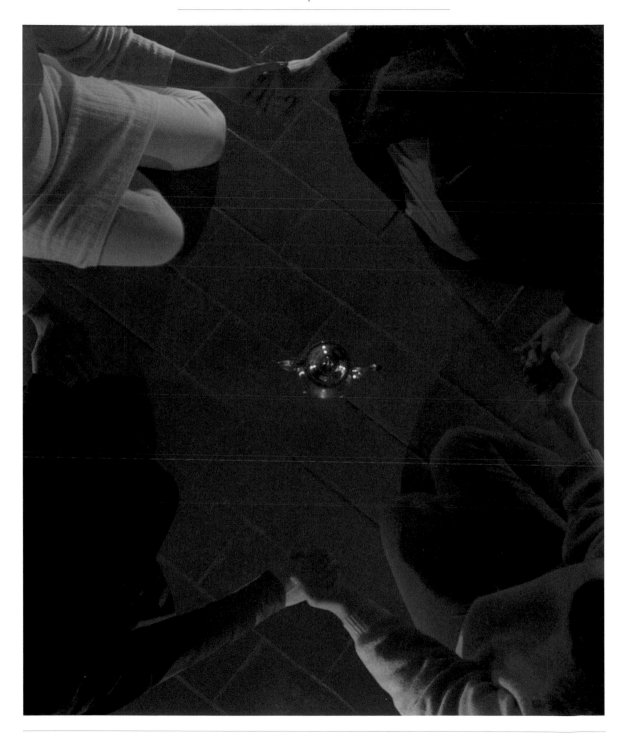

Nephitis is the sister of the Egyptian goddess Isis, and represents the female sex.

prepare this philtre you can all hold hands around the potion, with the candles extinguished, in the dark, sending your strength to the potion: this will make it more potent yet.

Now pour some of the liquid into your flask. Remove the pearl. Throw away the remaining brew into living water (the sea, the river, a pond or stream).

It is done.

The Magic of Key N° 8

This philtre will help you find the "real woman" inside you. Against all stereotypes, against all impositions and fears, against all male-imposed ideals, you will find the truth of your womanliness: what it means, for you, to be a woman.

This truth will shine forth and your hair will shine, your skin will be soft and your eyes luminous. You will know beauty like never before, and the strength and positive power of your own sex. You will love and be loved and feel that it is, finally, really you who is giving and receiving.

MAGIC KEY N° 9
Man's Magic

Ingredients

1. AMERICAN GINSENG
(Panax Quinquefolium)

This plant is found in hardwood forests, where the earth is very rich and humid. It is found in wild regions of Maine and Minnesota, and in the mountains of Georgia and Arkansas.

The root of ginseng is the important part of the plant. It is big and fleshy and after the second year it forks, taking on the characteristic aspect of a human form.

Eastern man has used this plant for thousands of years to give him strength and virility. Modern medicine is just beginning to discover that in fact ginseng appears to possess many beneficial properties and is rich in many essential vitamins and minerals.

The best way to take ginseng is to chew little bits of the root, or to make an infusion with them, then drink the liquid and chew the pulp.

Ginger is a strong tonic which heats the blood,
speeds up the metabolism, and has long been used
as an aphrodisiac.

For the Love Philtre we will use a fresh ginseng root.

2. NASTURTIUM

Nasturtium is a climbing plant with important, strongly colored flowers, which range from yellow to deep orange. It is originally from Peru and China, but it is now very popular in Europe. It flowers from April to September, and must be seeded every season in the spring. It is very easy to keep nasturtium in the garden, or even in pots on a windowsill.

Use seeds, leaves and flowers to make an infusion, which is very beneficial for colds and bronchitis as it eliminates mucus.

Take the flowers fresh if you can, or dry them by hanging in a well-aired, dark room.

3. WALNUT

The walnut was originally an Eastern tree, but it is found now everywhere in the western countryside. According to the Kama Sutra the walnut can give virility to any man, and also the ancient Romans were very impressed with the aphrodisiac properties of the walnut!

For the potion we use a handful of leaves from a walnut tree, taken during a full Moon. To be able to extract full power from the philtre the tree must not be found near a street transited by vehicles, but in a quiet country location.

4. GINGER

This spice is a strong tonic, which heats the blood, speeds up the metabolism, and is an aphrodisiac. The ancient Egyptians used it as a massage aid for sex — and they certainly knew about ingredients that "keep" things for a long time!

For the potion we use a fresh ginger root, grated.

Procedure

This philtre is to be prepared by men only (just as the previous one was prepared by women only). The presence of a

Below. Leaves from the walnut tree.
Right: The consuming element of Fire adds potency to the Man's Magic Philtre.

woman during the preparation of this philtre would spoil it, and you would have to start over again.

If possible, find yourself in a house which has either a fireplace or the possibility to make a bonfire outside. Have your utensils with you: the copper pots, the teapot, the spoon and strainer and the flask.

Take the ginseng root and two cups of water, and boil it for at least 15 minutes in the copper pot for herbs.

Powder the dry walnut leaves and add two tablespoons full to the boiling pot, together with a pinch of grated ginger.

Left: Straining the liquid obtained from simmering
nasturtium flowers into the teapot.
Below: Dried and powdered walnut leaves and a pinch
of grated ginger, ingredients in the discovery of the
"inner man."

Turn off the fire and let the mixture sit.

In the meantime take the copper pot for flowers and simmer a handful of nasturtium flowers in one cup of water, for two minutes. Strain the liquid into the teapot.

Strain the contents of the ginseng mixture also into the teapot. Add half a glass of very strong red wine and stir with the silver spoon.

After it is well stirred, take the concoction (still in the teapot) to the fireplace or the bonfire and let it sit there while you (with your male friends if you wish) stare at the flames and pronounce the words of magic:

To the Man's Fire
To the Lover's Pyre.

You can all drink from the wine while you are doing this: but once you are finished, if there is still some wine in the bottle you must throw it into the flames and break the bottle on the stone of the fireplace, or the power of the potion will be diminished.

Pour the philtre into the flask, throw into the flames any remaining liquid.

The Magic of Key Nº 9

"Man's Magic" will help man to reach his own inner strength and love. It grants virility, grounding, and a sense of well-being. It takes you "out of your head" (your worries, preoccupations) and puts you into your body.

This philtre taken before a night of passion will take you into the early hours of the morning; in conjunction with Dream Magic it will show you ways of discovering what your "inner man" is truly like, what he wants and desires and what can fulfill his heart.

If you are, like many, a man who finds that sex and love are difficult to find together in one nourishing relationship, try taking this Magical Key in conjunction with both the Fire and the Water element.

PART VIII

Love, Magic at Work

Just the fragrance of melissa oil can help you to prepare
for that all-important meeting with a new lover.

Now you have all the tools and information you need to perform your Love Magic. As you grow more familiar with the Nine Magical Keys, the qualities of the Four Elements, and the Magic of the Moon, you will grow more expert in mixing all these ingredients together into a truly effective magic practice.

In the meantime, to help you get started, I have outlined in this section some of the dilemmas common to lovers, and the magic I have used in dealing with them.

Magic to Prepare for a Love Meeting

You are at a party, a fascinating photographer has been talking to you and claims that he would love to take your portrait. From the way he is looking at you, you believe that it is a lot more than a photograph that he would like to take of you. You like the idea, but just as you are getting excited...your face starts flushing very bright red!

Or: You have just obtained a much longed for rendezvous with the most beautiful girl in town. Of course you are happy, but you are also terribly apprehensive: what impression are you going to make on her? How can you appear at your best? And just what are you going to do about the fact that every time you are nervous your palms sweat!

These are cases where a little Melissa Magic will help you go a long way.

Prepare for magic as you usually do, and burn in the essence burner three drops of melissa oil floating on water. Call the elements. Let's say the element Water answers you.

Before your meeting, you will take a bath

Visualizing a burning flame that starts at the navel is part
of the magic of awakening the body to sensuality.

in which you have dispersed six drops of melissa essential oil. While in the water concentrate on the situation at hand and say these words:

> *Melissa suffice
> for strength
> and for peace*

See yourself relaxed and at ease, holding hands without becoming sweaty, holding a gaze without blushing. You will know the magic of melissa is working because you will be able to imagine this easily and effortlessly, whereas normally you have not even been able to do these things in your imagination.

Carry the essence with you in a small silver flask with a cork that is easily removable. When you feel the old jitters come back, slip away for a minute, concentrate yourself, uncork the bottle with your left hand, holding it with the right, inhale the scent and repeat the magic words to yourself three times.

Magic to Awaken the Body to Sensuality

Let's begin with an example, now, of specific magic derived from a consultation with the Magic Circle. A woman prepares the Circle, arranges the candles and the symbols of the elements, and asks a question related to how she can allow herself to enjoy her sensuality more fully. She is answered by being drawn to the element "Earth."

This woman would use neroli essence in conjunction with the Love Philtre "Woman's Magic." And she would perform a ritual at the appropriate time, using an Earth method, as indicated in the table of the elements on page 140.

First she chooses the right Moon, and decides that a full Moon in Taurus would be ideal (see page 131). On that night — or even a few days

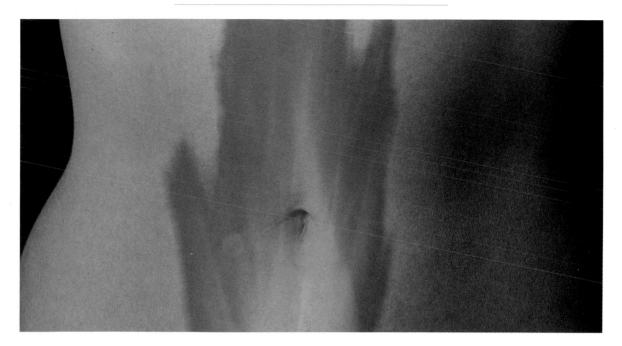

beforehand, in preparation — she surrounds herself with the color green. She can wear it, or make up her bed with it, or place a lot of plants around her house.

At the right time she massages neroli on her body, and prepares the "Woman's Magic" philtre. Then, after taking three sips of the philtre, she pours it into the special flask which she places around her neck, to reach the navel, saying these words:

By the magic of the Moon,
by the magic of Fire,
my body is consumed
with passion's desire.

And she envisions her body literally burning with a flame that starts at her navel, where the philtre lies. As with all magic, while pro-

nouncing the spell and visualizing, her focus must be complete and her attention and concentration totally absorbed in the action.

Magic to Open the Heart to Love

Bathing is a good method to follow for women who have dedicated long years to building up a career, with all the struggles involved, particularly for those working their way up the ladder of success. It often happens that such a woman one day feels that her heart has become closed to the lure of love: there has never been any time left for long walks in a park with a lover, never the space for lying in until midday, listening to each other's heartbeats.

Jasmine magic can bring her back to the life of love and passion, it can make the

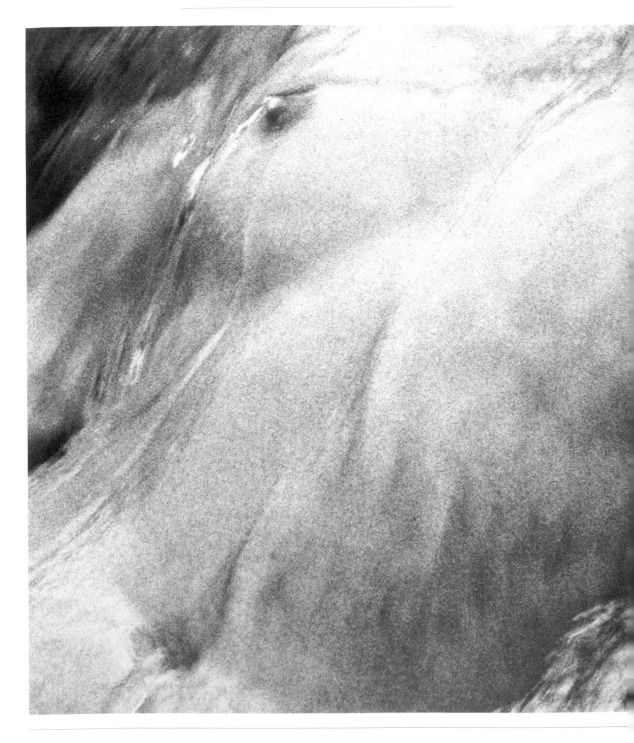

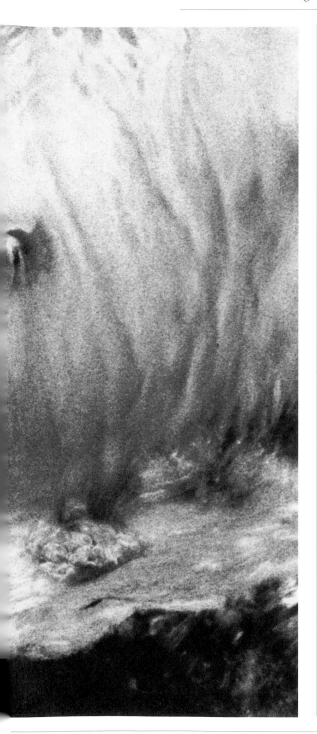

Bathe by the light of
three blue candles
to awaken the heart
to love.

heart's walls crumble...and without causing her to miss one single company meeting!

This is a magic ritual ruled by Water, so it will start with a waxing Moon in a Water sign (best of all Cancer) and will be complete with the next full Moon in a Water sign. If you enjoy the ritual and feel like carrying it on for some time, the magic grows strongest of all if you continue until the Moon is full in the same sign in which you have started.

During the time you are practicing this ritual, whenever possible, you will surround yourself with the color blue — not a dark blue, though — and will always have by the bed a silver cup filled with fresh wine, or water, in homage to the element Water.

Each night you will put three drops of jasmine essence in your bathwater, then switch off all electric lights so that you can bathe by the light of three blue candles. On those nights when the light of the Moon is sufficient, you can dispense with the candles and let the moonlight bathe you together with the essence of jasmine.

By the time of the next watery full Moon

and the tree was re...
tall, all the way at the...
top the branches got very...
thin... limb all the way
to ...and it was
ver... because
the ... branch...
one could...

The essence of rose on your forehead before you go to sleep can bring dreams of a new love in your life. Remember to write down the dreams when you wake up.

there will be an invitation which you can accept for pleasure, and not for business, or a night spent in loving with no thought or worry about what your schedule holds for tomorrow.

One word of advice: if you find that you are very nervous at the idea of a love meeting (the first one after such a long time!) take a few sips of the Magic Key N° 5, the Love Philtre for a love meeting, and all will be well.

Dream Magic for a Love to Appear in Your Life

If you are asking for a lover in your life, use the essence of rose in conjunction with Dream Magic.

The full Moon in Aquarius is the best for this one, but any other full Moon in an Air sign will work well.

Using the oil, anoint your forehead with a symbol of the eye before going to sleep. As you are about to drift off, ask your "dream guide"

The True Perception Love Philtre and the tiger eye, stone of self-confidence, can help in making the difficult decision of whether or not to commit to a relationship.

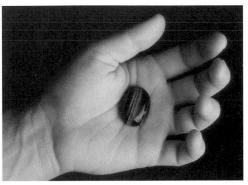

to show you the paths which lead to a lover in your life. Keep a notebook and pen next to your bed. Just putting the the notebook and pen there will help you to remember the dreams you are given, and you will be able to write them down as soon as you wake up, without the disturbance of getting out of bed and searching for them.

You might dream of swimming: look around you next time you go to a pool or to the seaside — your future lover could be the swimmer next to you! Or you could dream of going to the hairdresser. Your dream guide is telling you to spruce up your appearance, so that your lover will have an easier time finding you!

Magic for Deciding Upon a Commitment

A friend of mine, David, had been in a relationship for quite some time. He liked the woman well enough, sex between them was great, and her obvious beauty attracted him strongly. But he always seemed on edge, never quite at ease with his life. The two of them had moved in together, and in the four months since they had made that decision he had moved out — and then back in again — four times! His girlfriend was getting to the point where she would have no more of it. And David, too, was anxious to come to grips with what was causing him to behave in this hurtful way.

Sitting in the Magic Circle, the element which answered him was Fire. The tarot card he chose was The Chariot. At the root of his behavior the issue was one involving his very life energy, his vitality; it was an issue of what he wanted to do with himself (Fire). To this, the card of The Chariot added its message:

"You need to take yourself into your own hands, and not let outside considerations or momentary whims determine what you do right now. Ask yourself, without any preju-

If you are doing what you really want to be doing, stay with it. If not, change direction, no matter what others say.

dices, if you are doing what you really want to be doing. If yes, stay with it, without worrying about others. If not, change direction. You have the strength, power and courage to make what you want of your life."

I gave him the Magic Key N° 6, the Love Philtre for True Perception, to take using a Fire method.

Fortunately the full Moon in the same sign of his birth Moon was only a week away — and it was a Moon in Leo, a Fire sign. There was certain to be a lot of strength behind this magic!

On the night he was to perform his Love Magic, David went to the house of a friend who lived in the countryside. The house had a beautiful fireplace, which was just what David needed for his ritual. And, in the countryside the Moon is so clearly visible, so vivid and present...it was a perfect setting to take advantage of the happy coincidence that the Moon was full in Leo, which was also the sign of his natal Moon. It was an event which, under other circumstances, might not have happened at all in a year's time!

At midnight David went outside and, under the full Moon, standing on the grass,

A little Love Magic can put the spark back in a
relationship that has fallen into habits and routines.

he drank three sips from the philtre. Then,
coming back inside he threw the remaining
liquid into the fire in the fireplace, while visualizing himself burning symbolically in the
flames. Then he went to bed holding a tiger
eye (a stone for self-confidence) in his left
hand.

By the next morning David, without even
thinking about it, had no more doubts about
what he wanted.

He said, "It was just like waking up from a
dream. I couldn't understand anymore what
all the fuss had been about. I knew what I
wanted to do, and I just did it, feeling
absolutely ordinary about it."

David moved out of his girlfriend's house
for the last time. In fact, at that point, she was
quite relieved to see him go. She soon found a
man who was stable and happy to be with
her, and David began to enjoy a very carefree
time in his life. He had finally found the energy (and the courage) to be light and playful,
having lots of friends and — many! — girlfriends.

A couple of years later he settled down
with a woman, and this time there was no
wavering about his decision.

Magic to Rekindle Love Feelings

If your relationship has been dragging for a
while, and you wish to rekindle the sparkle of
love, use the rose essence in your burner during lovemaking. And to make it even more
powerful fill the room with roses, and invest
in a set of pink satin sheets. Make the best use
of the next full Moon in a Fire sign.

In the most intimate moment, when your
bodies are alive with pleasure and your
minds open and relaxed, murmur this in your
lover's ear:

Awake, awake,
your heart mine,
for Moon and love
they intertwine.

"What did you say my darling?" your lover
will probably ask. You just answer: "That I
love you very much."

This will be enough, s/he will be passion-
ately yours for many more Moons.

A waning Moon in the earliest hours of the morning, under a big tree... the perfect time and place for magic to help your real beauty to surface.

Magic for Your Beauty to Surface

If you are a woman who has trouble feeling good about your physical appearance use Woman's Magic in conjunction with the Earth element. The Magic Key N° 8 will help you to "let go" of all the attitudes you have about your looks, so that your own real beauty can again surface.

The Moon to choose for this will be a waning Moon (to help you in letting go) in an Earth sign (Taurus, Virgo or Capricorn). The color to be surrounded by and to wear is green.

Find a place for yourself outside, under a big tree that inspires you, dressing yourself in a green mantle under the Moon and the stars. The last quarter of the waning Moon is visible during the second half of the night and early morning. Around five o' clock in the morning will be a good time for this magic as the Moon will be high in the sky and the Earth will just be waking up from a night's sleep.

Take the flask containing the philtre and

> Love Magic can help us to understand more about our unconscious attitudes towards sexuality — attitudes that may be preventing us from fully enjoying the sensual pleasures of love.

drink of it three times, looking to the Moon with the first sip, to the Earth with the second, and to the Moon again with the third.

Like the Earth awakening so is my body!

Say these words three times, one for each sip of the philtre.

Pour the remaing liquid into the ground, very slowly. While you are doing this, visualize all your old ideas about your appearance disappearing into the Earth as the liquid is absorbed by the soil.

Magic to Discover the Origin of Sexual Fears

Anna, the wife of one of my cousins, is a pleasant woman of about forty years of age. She is dark and plump and looks a lot younger than her age. Alfredo and Anna have been married for only two years, but their love life never worked well. Half seriously, Anna asked me if I had a solution for her problem. I told her to use the Magic Key N° 2, in conjunction with the element Air (understanding) and Dream Magic. She reported

A little bit of ylang-ylang in conjunction with the element
Air and your body can speak of its true sexual nature.

this dream to me after performing ylang ylang magic:

"I suddenly woke up in the middle of the night with the very vivid dream, so vivid it could have been real, that a big mouse was moving around my neck, between my head and shoulders. The animal scuttled about a bit before running away. I woke up in utter panic and it took me a while before I was able to convince myself that I was in my own bed, where there was no possibility of a mouse coming near me."

I hope no such frightening occurrence will happen to you with your magic! Yet this one was very interesting and it did help Anna a great deal. You must know that in Italian slang "la topa," the mouse, (female) is one of the names for the vagina, the female sex organ. At the same time, for women especially, this animal inspires great fear and disgust: it seems to be dirty, it is furry, and "it moves." Anna, due to her upbringing, thought of her sexual feelings as separate from herself, as having a life of their own (it moves!), as dirty, as disgusting and frightening.

In fact Anna has a very sexual nature, and her whole body speaks of it — her body though, not her mind. She had made a division between her body and her head — that was why the mouse was sitting there, at the neck. And she operated in her life from her head, trying to control the horrible beast below the neck — her body and the sex that spoke through her body. But in the process she had hurt her own heart, too. Trying to "make use" of her body from her head she had often ignored the cries of the heart within the body.

After the ylang-ylang ritual Anna, with her lover and the help of Love Magic, has begun her own healing.

Magic to Raise Your Sexual Potential

A couple came to know me and my magic on a holiday we happened to share in the Swiss mountains. Karl and Wilma were two lovely people, very lively and curious. One evening we had been sitting cosily together in front of the fire, and had had a drink or two. I think this prompted them to open the subject of sex.

Essence of neroli, and red, the color of passion...
ingredients for a magical night of loving.

Lively though they were, I don't think that they would otherwise have started talking about it with me, after all, a stranger.

They said that though they had enjoyed it all their life together, they were sure that there could be more to it, but they just did not know how to go about it. Being intelligent they had already figured out that all the sexual manuals full of different positions would not give them what they were after.

I told them to try the Magic Key N° 1, the Sex Opener, in conjunction with the element Fire:

Prepare your bedroom by extinguishing all electric lighting and placing red candles around the room. Place an essence burner at the foot of your bed and put three drops of Neroli of Melangola in the water. Have red flowers and red fruits everywhere in the room, so that the sweet scent of the flowers and the aroma of the fruits will mix and mingle with the neroli scent.

Then I explained to them how to prepare themselves as is explained on page 68. And once prepared, to follow these instructions:

Holding the hand of your partner, face the direction of the Moon. Inhale three times the sweet scent of neroli and feel a deep relaxation come into every cell of your body. Holding hands, sitting down (either at the edge of the bed, or on a carpet or cushion under the window), let the Moon's rays shine on you, and the warm flicker of the candles cast shadows on you. After you have been sitting like this for no less than three minutes, say these words together: (If you do not want to learn them by heart, you can read them together aloud from a paper on which you will have previously written them.)

*By this Moon
and this scent for sure
I feel my body more passion endure.*

Then caress and touch each other as long as you like — talking if you wish, or being silent

Often a tickle and a bit of laughter are what is needed
when the body tenses up against sexual energy instead
of opening towards it.

— all the time remaining relaxed. This should be your main focus: while giving pleasure to the other, you are also ensuring that s/he is still very relaxed. The attention should never waver from this point, which is as important as the giving of pleasure, if not more important.

While kissing the face see that the jaw is relaxed, when caressing soothe away tension from the shoulders. And if the hands of your lover come into a fist, open them and kiss the palms to make them wide again. Often a tickle and a bit of laughter are what is needed when the body tenses up against the sexual energy instead of opening up towards it. This will be easy to do when you are surrounded by the sweet magic of neroli and the soft presence of the Moon.

If you ever feel that you are losing your relaxed attentiveness, all you need to do is to look at the Moon again, inhale the scent, and repeat the magic words once more.

With the help of magic you will be able to reach higher and higher peaks of pleasure while remaining relaxed, and in this way the final fulfillment will come out of your own choice. Then it will be a cascade of pure ener-

gy and joy, in which you will feel more than ever the magic that is in you and around you.

Indeed, sex is the life-creating ritual; in itself it contains the roots of all magic. Approaching sex with a relaxed attitude and with love, and with the help of the magic of nature, you can go to those very roots where you will find answers for all your questions and fulfillment for your whole being.

Magic to Heal Old Love Wounds

Some people seem to have come to this Earth already equipped with a good dose of heart pain. As children they cling desperately to their mother's skirts and cry for no reason. When they grow up they are determined to prove to themselves that love hurts, and they surely succeed. After the first strong experience of rejection they retreat back into themselves, satisfied to have proved the "truth" of their expectation.

Do you recognize yourself? I was one such person, until I remembered my family's teachings and decided to use magic to heal myself.

Maybe you were a happy, trusting soul until the day
you met one of those alluring individuals whose sole
purpose in life seems to be to add one more "trophy"
to their collection!

Or maybe you were a happy, trusting soul until the day you met one of those charming, alluring individuals whose sole purpose in life seems to be to add one more "trophy" to their collection... He, or she, destroyed your happiness and you have since retreated into a shell of suspicion.

Or, even, it was nobody's fault — you are not bitter or resentful, you can even be friends with the person who caused you pain....but the memory of the hurt is so vivid and frightening that you dare not try it again.

In all these cases and, so I think, for the better part of mankind, the following ritual can be a turning point.

As this is such an important issue it is well worth waiting for an appropriate lunar phase. The best thing is to wait until the Moon is passing through your birth sign: that is, if your natal Moon is in Pisces, you will wait until the next time the Moon is full in that sign. However, since the Moon is full in each sign just once a year, you might have to wait too long for that. Alternatively, you can use a night when the Moon is full in one of the Water signs — Scorpio, Pisces, or Cancer. Since this is a Water ritual, a watery Moon

will be well aspected. (Remember that two days before and two days after a full Moon can be used for full Moon magic, as explained on page 125).

Place four light blue candles in your silver candleholders and put them at the four corners of your bathtub. Change the light bulb in your bathroom to a blue-colored one for this evening. And if you already have them, or if you can afford to buy them now, have a matched set of blue towels. Find blue flowers and arrange them also in your bathroom.

Proceed with this ritual when everybody else is asleep (provided that the Moon is visible, of course). The middle of the night is a good time for this magic: it is the time when old pains surface again and you can naturally feel the hurt in your heart. Usually you try to switch it off — maybe you would get up and watch TV, or eat, or read, or all the three together! This time you will stay with the feeling in your heart, without any fear, because you know you are safe within the strong, soft arms of the magic world.

Place the scent burner in the bathroom with two drops of jasmine oil. Run the bathwater to a comfortable heat, and when the

A healing bath in blue candlelight to wash away old love wounds. A pink quartz held in the hand as you fall asleep, and your dreams will help your heart to heal.

bath is full add four drops of jasmine oil. If you are doing this ritual when jasmine is in flower you can let as many as seven or nine little flowers float on the surface of the water.

Stay in the water with closed eyes until you feel relaxed. Breathe in the scent of the jasmine and feel the air go into your heart, soothing, caressing, warming. Whatever emotions might come up, do not try to understand. (If you feel sadness, for example, you might be tempted to explain the feeling to yourself: "I must be feeling this way because B. did not return my calls.") Instead, just let the feeling be there. Say these words aloud three times:

In you, jasmine, my body I feel.
In you, jasmine, my heart I heal.

As with all spells, when you pronounce a spell you must be totally focused on the words you are saying.

Stop if the feeling gets too uncomfortable. There can be a lot of pain in one's heart, and it is not possible sometimes to heal it all at once.

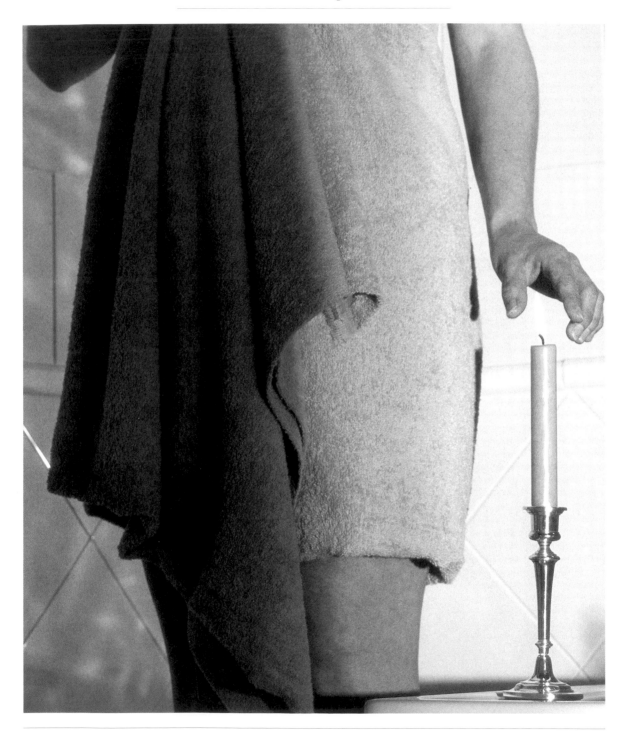

Pinch out the candles, without looking back at the water.

Get out of the bath and wrap yourself in the blue towel, being careful not to glance back at the water. Closing your eyes, pinch out the candles and go to your bed.

It is very likely that if you have a partner and sleep with him or her, the effect of the jasmine magic will wake him up and draw him/her to you. Welcome the lovemaking as that will add energy to your magic. The quality of sex in this moment, if you have a sensitive partner, will be warm and healing.

Fall asleep holding a pink quartz in your hand — it is the healing stone. In the night you will probably have dreams. They might be scary ones, painful ones, sad ones. It is your heart unburdening itself. Pay close attention to your dreams and write them down in the morning. As you review them from time to time you will be able to recognize what hints your unconscious is giving you to help your heart heal.

Magic for a Choice in Love

Jay was a young man of about 25 years of age. Very intelligent and well dressed, he lived in town and had two full-time girlfriends — one in the same town where he lived, the other one in the next. Jay lived a double life and was not too happy about it: it was wearing him down, but it seemed to him that he could not find a way out of it because, really, he wanted both women and did not want to let go of either of them. The first one he loved, or so he thought; the second one he had fabulous sex with, or so it seemed to him.

When he came to me and sat in the Magic Circle, funnily enough he felt that there were two elements calling out to him, and not just one! The two elements were, just so, Fire and Water.

When I asked him to choose a card, he pulled out The Lovers.

Through this card I realized that Jay, in spite of having two simultaneous affairs, was longing for real love. Although he thought he was in love with both women, he really had not opened his heart to either one of these two girls. The only way for him to finally fall in love was to reunite the sex and the heart energies within himself.

I gave him the recipe for preparing the "Man's Magic" philtre, to be taken at the next

Who do I really love?
Magic can help us see the answer clearly.

transit of the Moon through the sign of his natal Moon. These were his instructions:

"Take a burner and make a fire with pure birch wood. Next to it place a large silver bowl containing pure spring water. When you are focused and calm, sit between the two — the fire on your right, the water on the left. Take the flask with the philtre and drink twice. Then with the left hand pour some into the water, with the right hand pour some into the fire.

"Now sit silently — the only light will be that of the fire and of the Moon. Stretch out your hands, palms upwards towards the two elements. Feel the powers of Water and Fire as they flow through your hands, through your arms and into your body. Stay focused on this sensation. Then put your attention simultaneously on your sexuality and your heart. This can be difficult to do, take your time. When you have achieved this focusing you will see a white light, maybe in the shape of a lotus, which appears in the middle of you, at about the height of the navel.

"The appearance of the Lotus, or white light, can be so powerful as to seem like an inner explosion, and send you flying backwards, so that you end up flat on your back.

"This is the meeting of the sacred and the profane, of the love for the flesh, with the love for the soul. That same night go to sleep holding a quartz crystal in your hand and you will dream of the woman whom you can love with all of yourself."

Jay did perform this magic, although he had to do it quite a few times before he was able to keep properly focused. The effect was quite powerful for him. He dreamed of both of his girlfriends. The first one took a photograph from a stand and smashed it on the floor: it was the photo of the wedding of his mother and father. The other one (the one he

Use lots of green everywhere — green food, green
bedding, green clothes, green lights, and plants.

had great sex with) in the dream was naked
and crying.

Jay woke up from the dream "knowing"
that with the first woman he was trying to
recapture the feelings he had watched
between his father and mother. They had
loved each other very much and a part of
him, growing up, wanted to repeat that experience. He did not truly love this woman for
what she was. With the second girl his dream
told him he was far more involved, and his
heart was crying out to be let into that affair.

This is what happened: Jay left the first
girl and dedicated himself to the second one
only. Soon he was truly in love with her and
very happy.

Magic to Dispel Old Wounds Caused by Violence

For this magic you need a very loving and
patient partner. You will be using the Sex
Healer, in connection with the element of
Earth.

Start with a
full Moon in an
Earth sign, and
proceed until
the black Moon
in an Earth sign.
You will have one
sitting every night
when the Moon is waning
in an Eearth sign, until the final night of the
black Moon. The whole magic process will
take two or three months, with two or three
sittings per month.

Use a lot of green everywhere. Green food,
green bedding, green clothes, green lights,
and plants. Buy green candles and keep one
burning by the bed all the time that you are
practicing the magic. If you can find a little
jade statue place it in the bathroom as your
"Body Protector" (see page 45). Jade brings
beauty and helps you see the beauty of your
own body. Often people who have been sub-
jected to violence find themselves ugly.

For this magic, which is a strong and deli-
cate one, make sure to pay attention to
preparing yourselves really well. It is important to be relaxed and centered and focused.

By the time the black Moon comes into an Earth sign,
your lover will be ready to let go completely of the
pain and fear.

Greet the Moon and the element Earth by acknowledging their presence with the following ritual words:

Under the soft eye of Moon,
I greet you Earth,
who gives body to my passion.

Keep a silver bowl filled with fruit representing the Earth on the Love Altar or next to the bed while you are doing the magic.

The room must be warm and you can use many candles so you will have good lighting for the massage.

While you touch the body of your beloved concentrate on the area between the navel and the knees: that is, the belly and buttocks and thighs. Only touch the genitals if you can do so in a very relaxed way, without excitement.

Touch gently but firmly, in any way you like. You do not need to be a certified masseur for magic. The important thing is that your energy and the energy of your lover mingle together with the essence of ylang-ylang, the Moon and the Earth.

A few minutes will be enough — but you can of course proceed as long as you feel like it, provided that you stay "present" to your lover.

While you are touching the body of your lover say these words, three times:

The green of peace,
the scent of love,
the pain is past, in Earth at last.

You might feel like making love afterwards, or your partner might just want to rest and cuddle up with you, or maybe even cry.

By the time the black Moon comes in an Earth sign, your lover will be ready to let go completely of her pain and fears.

After the massage this time dress yourself up (wearing at least one green garment), take a piece of old clothing of a dark color and burn it outside, (drive out of town if you need to) in the black night.

A final word...

The examples I have given above, if they fit with your situation, can be used without first consulting with the Magic Circle of Love. They have been developed in many years of magic practice, and I have seen the magical results, so I know that they work.

Touch gently but firmly, in any way you like. You do not need to be a certified masseur for magic.

But if there is any feeling of hesitation, any small voice that whispers, "Yes, but my situation is just a little different..." then you must follow your own feeling. Perhaps the key to reawakening your sensuality lies with the Water element, and not the Earth. Or your inability to choose between two loves in your life comes from a misunderstanding, and it is the Air element that can help you.

In these cases, it is best that you take your situation to the Magic Circle of Love, and let the Moon and the cards guide you, allow the elements to help you, and trust your intuition to tell you which of the Nine Magical Keys to use. Finally, when performing the ritual indicated by all these magic tools, you can make up your own incantations and spells. I use rhymes because I enjoy them, and they are easy to remember, but it is not necessary. The only important thing is that the words express your true wishes and feelings.

Your sincerity — and your playfulness! — will ensure that you cannot go wrong.

The Spring of Love

RITUAL	ELEMENT	MAGICAL KEY
To awaken the body to sensuality	Earth	N° 1 and N° 8
To open your heart to love	Water	N° 4
For a lover to appear in your life	Air	N° 3
To prepare for a love meeting	Water Air	N° 5
For your beauty to surface	Earth	N° 8

COLOR	METHOD	MOON	PAGE
Green	Massaging and wearing	Full Moon in Taurus	178
Blue	Bathing	Waxing in Cancer to full in a Water sign	179
Yellow	Dreaming	Full in Aquarius	183
Yellow Blue	Bathing and inhaling	New Moon in an Air sign	176
Green	Pouring in the earth and wearing	Waning in an Earth sign	191

Being Together

RITUAL	ELEMENT	MAGICAL KEY
To discover the origin of sexual fears	Air	N° 2
To raise your sexual potential	Fire	N° 1
To heal love wounds	Water	N° 4
To dispel wounds caused by violence	Earth	N° 2

COLOR	METHOD	MOON	PAGE
Yellow	Dream	Full Moon in Libra	192
Red	Burning	Waxing Moon in a Fire sign	193
Blue	Bathing	Natal Moon, full or full Water Moon	196
Black	Massaging	Full to black in an Earth sign	204

Settling Down

RITUAL	ELEMENT	MAGICAL KEY
To rekindle love feelings	Fire	Nº 3
For deciding upon commitment	Fire	Nº 6
For a choice in love	Fire Water	Nº 9
Jealousy	Air	Nº 7
Ending a love affair	Fire	Nº 6

COLOR	METHOD	MOON	PAGE
Red	Essence burning	Full in a Fire sign	188
Red	Burning	Full in Leo	185
Red Blue	Burning Drinking	Natal Moon, any phase	201
Yellow	Spellmaking	Waning Moon in Libra	
Red	Burning	Black Moon, any sign	

PART IX

Astrological Help for Overcoming Difficulties

When you have an understanding of your partner's
strengths and weaknesses, you can use this knowledge to
avoid stormy and unpleasant scenes.

Astrology is one of the most ancient tools of wise men and women. The knowledge of the influence of the stars on human life, just as the knowledge of the influence of herbs and flowers, of colors, numbers, and symbols, is essential to the practice of magic.

In the practice of Love Magic we can learn much from two important planets in our solar system, Venus and Saturn. Venus is the planet that rules the aspect of love expressed as giving and sharing. Saturn, on the other hand, represents the blocks and hindrances which impede the free flow of love, and must be cleared in order to allow the love energy to circulate without obstruction. Both aspects of love are essential to the workings of human relationships. Without Venus there would be no pleasure in loving, and without Saturn there would be no growth.

Each one of us has both these aspects of love in our astrological make-up. Both Venus and Saturn are there, in the sky, at everyone's birth. By determining the exact position of these two planets at the moment you were born, there is much that you can learn about your strengths and weaknesses in love rela-

tionships. And when you also have an understanding of your partner's strengths and weaknesses, you can use this knowledge to avoid some of the more stormy and unpleasant scenes that can happen when two people react blindly to each other for reasons "beyond their control."

In this section, we take a look at how Venus and Saturn express their influence within the different elements and their astrological signs. For the sake of simplicity in the descriptions that follow, I have chosen Venus to represent the female lover in the relationship and Saturn the male. But keep in mind that both planets exist in your chart, and both of them influence your love affairs. So both men and women should read information about both Venus and Saturn in their own charts, and in the charts of their lovers.

Venus in a Fire Sign
(Aries, Leo, Sagittarius)
MEETING WITH
Saturn in a Fire Sign

A fiery Venus is a "hot" lover. She is strong and independent, her love is warm and pas-

Understanding the influence of the stars on human life is
essential to the practice of magic.

sionate. She knows little fear and can immerse herself totally, without holding back, in the care and nourishing of another person.

On the other side, the fear of "letting go" is the biggest problem for those who have Saturn in Aries, Leo, or Sagittarius. If your partner is a fiery Saturn, know well that no matter how hard he may try to hide it, deep down he is afraid of the experience we call "love." Trust is the quality he has been destined to learn: trust in himself, trust in the fact that he is worthy of love, trust in the gifts that existence is ready to bestow on him through the warmth of his lover's heart.

VENUS IN ARIES — Beware of your enthusiasm and impulsiveness, for they could be misunderstood. Let your interest for your lover appear in a steady, reassuring, dependable light.

VENUS IN LEO — Don't try to become the center of your lover's world. Don't try to make decisions on his behalf, even if you are sure you are right and believe you are acting out of sincere generosity and love. Your respect for your lover's fears, and the example of your own energy and trust, are the best "gifts of the heart" you can offer.

VENUS IN SAGITTARIUS — Give your partner time to understand and surrender to love without interfering. There is nothing to be taught about matters of love through words. Be silent, be patient, be loving, and wait: you could lose your partner by trying to reach him more directly.

Venus in a Fire Sign
MEETING WITH
Saturn in a Water Sign
(Cancer, Scorpio, Pisces)

A partner with Saturn in Cancer, Scorpio, or Pisces is certainly one of the most challenging for a fiery Venus. A watery Saturn is usually associated with very painful emo-

A fiery Venus is a "hot" lover, strong and independent,
loving and passionate.

tional wounds, whose origins can often be found only in childhood. "Nobody ever loved me, nobody ever will" — this could be his motto. He has an unspoken, often unconscious belief underlying his compulsive defensiveness, a sense of unworthiness that is deeply connected with feelings, emotions, and their expression through sex, intimacy, and affection.

When they don't choose to simply hide away, watery Saturns may try very hard to behave like a Don Juan or a Hollywood vamp — the opposite of what he or she really feels! Whatever the case, remember that deep down you are dealing with a child who still hankers for reassurance, warmth, and emotional security.

Saturn, the Hard Master of Love, will eventually force your lover to lower his defenses and to expose his emotional wounds, so that they can be healed by the warmth of your love.

VENUS IN ARIES — You bring energy and action as a gift to your watery Saturn. A little insight into astrology and magic will help you avoid the mistake of making the first move. Wait until he is ready to open up on his own — too direct an approach could scare him, and you might succeed in reaching his body, but not his heart.

VENUS IN LEO — Beware of your self-assertiveness if you want to conquer a watery Saturn. Let him see your gentle and feminine side: always wait for him to ask for your help, and never try to impose it on him.

VENUS IN SAGITTARIUS — You are the most optimistic of lovers, so it is hard for you to understand why it is difficult for your watery Saturn to let go of his pain. It will happen on its own accord — the message here is...be patient!

Venus in a Fire Sign
MEETING WITH
Saturn in an Earth Sign
(Taurus, Virgo, Capricorn)

"Growing roots" is a must for the man with Saturn in one of the earthy signs (Taurus, Virgo, Capricorn). His need for security and control in the world around him is so compulsive and strong that in matters of love he may try to possess his beloved like a thing, in order to have something stable and firm to

People with Venus in a Water sign are the sweetest
lovers, absolutely at home in the world of emotions,
feelings, and romance.

hold on to. Or, he may choose to run away
and deny that anything like real love is possible at all. He can behave as if the only
things that matter and give him a sense of
being "somebody" are power, money and
prestige.

If your Venus is in Aries, Leo, or
Sagittarius, there is much you can do for your
partner. Through the natural fire of your
heart and your love of freedom you will be
able to show your beloved that the sense of
belonging he is trying to achieve has nothing
to do with money, position, or power, and
everything to do with feelings, trust, and surrender to love.

A person with a fiery heart cannot be
manipulated or bought. This Venus cherishes
her freedom and doesn't care too much for
possessions; she is also generous, and can be
a source of strength for the person she loves.

The partner with an earthy Saturn needs
that support and warmth, as well as the partner's example of freedom, because life is often
a struggle for him.

VENUS IN ARIES — You will safeguard
your freedom by resisting any attempt to be
controlled. You can be affectionate and loving

in a free and giving way. Avoid being too
impatient and too uncompromising.

VENUS IN LEO — You can be generous
beyond any expectation, because you value
love more than anything else. What you can
give your earthy Saturn is total and unconditional support: a help he badly needs, because
life is often such a struggle for him. But do
not ask for too much in exchange for your
gifts; and if you see that your partner is not as
noble and inspired as you are...don't despise
him!

VENUS IN SAGITTARIUS — Be careful of
your tendency to move away too quickly
when waters get rough, or when you are disappointed; your earthy Saturn is a steady one,
and you need to be patient with his slow
moves. Share with him your sense of adventure.

Venus in a Fire Sign
MEETING WITH
Saturn in an Air Sign
(Gemini, Libra, Aquarius)

If you are interested in someone with Saturn
in Gemini, Libra or Aquarius you are dealing

Those with Saturn in an Air sign tend to be loners
at heart, who have trouble relaxing when other people
are around.

with someone who at heart is a loner. He may try to deny his true nature, pretending that he is a perfectly sociable person, lovable and charming. It is no use: if you watch him you will quickly realize that he is never really at ease when he is talking to you, that he can never relax with people around.

His problem is communication. He is too identified with his personal world to be able to open up to others, even when the other is the person he loves. He tends to be too rational and serious. Simplicity, non-seriousness, and a more easy-going state of mind are the qualities this Saturn must learn to integrate in his being in order to be happy and fulfilled in love and friendship.

VENUS IN ARIES — You can be a shining example of boldness and initiative. Your lover will admire your ability to be the center of attention without feeling tense or worried. But you should not demand that your Saturn partner behaves like an extrovert if he doesn't feel like it!

VENUS IN LEO — Your gift is the integrity and wholeness of the person who knows how to love herself. People are likely to give you a lot of attention. Be careful not to misuse

the power this attention can give you — your airy Saturn will not take it kindly!

VENUS IN SAGITTARIUS — Your sense of adventure is your gift to the earthy Saturn: you trust that you will always meet more friends than enemies. Avoid leaving your partner behind in your search for the new.

Venus in a Water Sign
(Cancer, Scorpio, Pisces)
MEETING WITH
Saturn in a Fire Sign
(Aries, Leo, Sagittarius)

People with Venus in the watery signs are the sweetest lovers. It is easy for them to create through their love a different kind of reality in which to invite their beloveds and to cherish them. The world of emotions, of feelings, romance and passion, is one in which they are absolutely at home. Their hearts contain a depth and intensity that can take them in a moment from ecstasy to pain, and back to ecstasy again. If they manage to fall in love without losing themselves altogether, with sincerity and without self-indulgence, they prove to be a real benediction for whoever

> Saturn represents the blocks and hindrances which impede the free flow of love, and which must be cleared in order to allow the love energy to circulate without obstruction.

needs emotional healing, or simply wants to put a song in his life.

We know how barren a person with Saturn in Fire can feel, who has forgotten his true spontaneity and clings to the rigid patterns of his personality. In the eyes of a lover with Venus in Water he will find the key to come out of his prison.

VENUS IN CANCER You can give your partner the feeling that he is needed, wanted, important. He doesn't have to hide and protect himself, and to play strong, because it is so clear that

you want him as much as he wants you. To be in love is as important to you as the air that you breathe, and you are grateful if your beloved is ready to receive your affection. Venus in Cancer is one of the sweetest and most tender combinations in the whole Zodiac. It gives you a great power, a loving magic that no one can resist.

Your gift is your vulnerability, your graceful surrender to love.

What you should avoid: being overprotective, or treating your lover like a child.

VENUS IN SCORPIO — Love for you means primarily passion and sexual attraction. When you are interested in a person, you keep pursuing them until you get what you want. Your presence has a very intense, sometimes even magnetic quality which could trigger the insecurities and fears of a person with Saturn in Fire.

However, you could be either very fulfilled or very disappointed with your fiery Saturn lover, because you give much and want much in return. Particularly you want sex to be much more than a biological function, rather it should express a deep merging that involves body, feelings and soul. If your Saturnine partner can trust and let go to that extent this can be the foundation for a durable relationship.

Your gift is the cool fire of your sexual energy and passion.

What you should avoid: being secretive.

Emotional fulfillment is very important in a
relationship...but you also need to learn how to live side
by side as mature, independent individuals.

VENUS IN PISCES — This combination can make you the most giving, fulfilled, and inspired of lovers, but it can also make you addicted to painful experiences and sad love affairs. In the first case you will have chosen a fiery Saturnine who has already learned his karmic lesson of letting go of his fears, and he will make you the happiest woman on earth. In the second case...he will keep on running away, and you will keep on crying.

The gift you bring to this relationship is the feeling of harmony with existence that you experience through love.

What you should avoid: masochism. You are better off without it.

Venus in a Water Sign
MEETING WITH
Saturn in a Water Sign

The match of people with Venus and Saturn in watery signs can prove a really good one, if the Saturnine partner is courageous enough to put his misery aside and open himself to the healing powers of his beloved. The only danger is that the two of them might fall too much into helping and being helped, and

thereby turn a beautiful and necessary healing process into an endless game. The charming prince should not wish that Sleeping Beauty falls asleep again and again, just so he can keep on waking her up with his kiss! Emotional fulfillment is a very important aspect of any relationship, but it is not all there is. The two partners here really fit with each other, but they should also learn how to live side by side as mature, independent individuals.

VENUS IN CANCER — Your heart will be like a safe haven where your partner can take shelter from the storms of life. You are really gifted in taking care of children and you like to have many around you. In the beginning of your relationship you will touch your lover's heart by seeing the needy child who hides inside him, afraid to come out. You will reassure him, you will create a beautiful home, and you will help him to grow and forget his fears. As we know, many people with Saturn in Water suffer from problems stemming from an unhappy childhood. As your relationship grows roots, your love will give your partner the chance of creating a new family and finding the happiness he did not have

Trust your feelings, but make sure that you are choosing
your partner for deeper reasons than just for the sake of
taking on an impossible challenge!

when he was small. Domestic happiness will be your gift. What you should avoid: don't forget there is more to life than your family and your house.

VENUS IN SCORPIO — You will prove to your partner that sex can be a beautiful act of love, rather than something dark and dangerous one should be afraid of. With Saturn in a Water sign, if your lover is a woman she has probably felt used and abused by men before meeting you. If he is a man he

might have experienced sex as a compulsion and a weakness, at the mercy of women who took material advantage of him and exploited his fears. You will show your beloved how to relax and let go in sex without fears and second thoughts: a beautiful foundation for a healthy and durable love affair. Your gift is your loving and intelligent approach to sex and intimacy. What you should avoid: don't go too fast. It may take some time before your lover can really be open to you.

VENUS IN PISCES — You may come across the kind of person who has been rejected and disappointed again and again each time has fallen in love, and has ended up embittered and alone as a result. Saturn in a Water sign often means that a person is unconsciously looking for total commitment, and unconditional love: a demand which would scare anyone except you, who have Venus in Pisces and know well that the heart knows no compromise or fear. Besides, you like impossible tasks, and the task of loving a person who can never get enough warmth and affection is certainly a difficult one!

Trust your feelings, but make sure that you are choosing your partner for deeper reasons and affinities rather than just for the sake of taking on an impossible challenge. Your gift consists of seeing love as an end in itself. What you should avoid: dropping your lover as soon as he is happy again!

If you have Venus in a Water sign, you like your partner
to be in charge of practical matters, and the earthy Saturn
will let you take care of his heart.

Venus in a Water Sign
MEETING WITH
Saturn in an Earth Sign
(Taurus, Virgo, Capricorn)

"Behind every great man there is always a great woman" — the reverse is also true. This applies unconditionally to the meeting of watery Venus and earthy Saturn. The earthy Saturn will be out there working, and the watery Venus will be in here nourishing.

If you have Venus in a Water sign you like your partner to be in charge of practical matters, and he will let you take care of his heart.

VENUS IN CANCER — You will insist that your partner does not sacrifice his best energies to his work. You would like him first of all to relax, take it easy, take care of himself, and of course take care of you. Your approach to life is soft and feminine, but you respect the courage and the stamina of your partner with Saturn in an Earth sign.

Your gift to him is your softness. What you should avoid: being too selfish in your demand for gentleness; what is good for you is not always good for others.

VENUS IN SCORPIO — You are the kind of person who can stand by her lover's side for better or worse: when you love you are not afraid of adversity, and people with Saturn in Earth often do meet with a lot of resistance in their striving for material success. Your sexual energy is powerful and can also heal. You will be there when he needs you.

Your gift is your respect for your partner. You are strong but you don't like to use people any more than you like them to use you.

What you should avoid: don't try to fulfill your desires whatever the cost.

VENUS IN PISCES — Your gift is your ability to merge and let go. What you should avoid: being lazy.

Venus in a Water Sign
MEETING WITH
Saturn in an Air Sign
(Gemini, Libra, Aquarius)

The meeting of Venus in a Water sign and Saturn in an Air sign is a challenge to go deeper than words — to find a common ground of understanding in silence, in feelings, in body

Watery Venus meeting airy Saturn is a challenge to go
deeper than words, to find a common ground of
understanding in silence, feelings, body language....

language, not just in superficial ideas or in everyday conversations. For the partner with Saturn in Air, as we know, communication is often a problem. Not that he does not know how to speak, or avoids the company of others — although sometimes this can be the case — he may be very skillful with words. But he rarely trusts himself and others enough to express what really matters to him, or the love he feels. For the partner with a watery Venus, on the other hand, the inner world of emotions means everything: she will never be satisfied unless she is certain of her beloved's feelings, and sure that her own feelings are being understood in return. The meeting of these two can bear beautiful fruit if they both realize that in matters of love, words communicate less than silence, and language can give just an illusion of communication rather than real sharing. Without that illusion it is easier, not more difficult, to love.

VENUS IN CANCER — You will feel protective and willing to take care of your solitary airy Saturn lover. For you, being in a relationship means above all to cultivate intimacy and mutual support: it will not be too big a sacrifice for you to do without too many people around, if you are really interested in your partner. You are not afraid of sadness and you can appreciate the silent beauty it sometimes gives to your beloved. Your gift is your tender care and understanding. What you should avoid: don't try to be understanding 24 hours a day. Sometimes it is good to be angry as well.

VENUS IN SCORPIO — You could feel attracted to both types of airy Saturn lovers: the one who copes with his problems by shunning company, and the other who tries to compensate by playing at being charming or seductive. With the former you can enjoy the pleasures that only undisturbed togetherness and sexual harmony can give. With the latter you could enjoy the challenge of being in a social situation with your lover without clinging to him or allowing him to cling to you, and proving that you can be as attractive and interesting as he is. In both cases your gift will be your passionate commitment to being true to your feelings: when you are in love you cannot just "behave yourself." What you should avoid: don't push too hard when there is something you want.

VENUS IN PISCES — You can bring light

Venus in an Earth sign gives the ability to provide
tangible evidence of the sincerity and depth
of your feelings.

into the life of any person you choose to love, and you instinctively seek the ones who need you most. You are like a cloud heavy with rain, longing to pour its water, and you like giving even more than receiving. Don't feel hurt if your airy Saturn partner tries to defend himself from you — he is afraid of your love. Before meeting you, he has probably suffered much at the hands of others and now he cannot conceive of the possibility of a relationship that is not based on exploitation. All you have to do is wait: time and your patience will heal his wounds. Your gift is your love and compassion. What you should avoid: don't become dependent on people needing your help.

Venus in an Earth Sign
(Taurus, Virgo, Capricorn)
MEETING WITH
Saturn in a Fire Sign
(Aries, Leo, Sagittarius)

If you have Venus in one of the earthy signs you have a natural ability to build solid foundations for your love affairs, to provide tangible evidence of the sincerity and depth of your feelings. This strength can do much to help your beloved come to terms with his fears and develop the ability to relax and enjoy the caring warmth of your presence.

The tangible evidence of your love can overcome the fears of even the most pessimistic of partners. In fact, the gift of the heart brought by Venus in the Earth signs is both self-evident and reliable. This Venus seldom promises in vain. She has much to share, and wants her beloved to get the best of what this world can give. She also knows what she wants and goes for it with perseverance and practical wisdom. Her desires are neither dreams nor whims.

VENUS IN TAURUS is one of the most beautiful combinations of the Zodiac in terms of sensuality, eroticism and warmth. Sex, food, beauty and richness are aspects of life that this Venus knows how to enjoy to their fullest, and she is eager to share these gifts with the object of her love. Pleasure and abundance cannot take the place of trust and relaxation, but they can certainly create the right climate for these qualities to flower.

Jealousy and possessiveness are what a person with Venus in Taurus should avoid.

Venus in Capricorn is a very powerful and austere force.
You can give your partner the feeling of being supported,
but be careful not to try to dominate or control.

Nobody likes to be owned like a thing: not even Saturn in a Fire sign, despite his fears.

VENUS IN VIRGO brings a gift of realism and rationality that would be a mistake to underestimate. A fiery Saturn really has a chip on his shoulder when it comes to the fear of being disillusioned and let down: a fear that always lurks in the hearts and minds of those who have suffered in the past and are afraid to open up once again. Venus in Virgo does not boast about her virtues. She will not promise everlasting passion; rather, she will work intelligently for a fulfilling and well-planned relationship without demanding open acknowledgment and appreciation. She will make sure that no unrealistic expectations ever come in the way of a healthy, nourishing relationship between two people who really complement each other. Here, the danger to avoid is that of being rational to the point of emotional coldness; this would kill what is most irrational and alive in your heart, and in the heart of your partner.

VENUS IN CAPRICORN brings a gift of sincerity, faithfulness and depth of feelings that is second to none. If this is your Venus you are not blind to the faults of your part-ners, and that's why your relationships generally last longer than those of many others. Before committing yourself you think twice, because when you choose someone you do it with the sincere intention of making this person part of your life for a long time. Being bossy and overpowering in matters of love is what you should avoid. The position of Venus in Capricorn is a very powerful and austere force. Your care and attention can give a person with Saturn in a fiery sign the feeling of being supported. But your attentions can become oppressive if they are used as part of an attempt to dominate or control your partner.

Venus in an Earth Sign
MEETING WITH
Saturn in a Water Sign
(Cancer, Scorpio, Pisces)

We have already seen how vulnerable, defensive, demanding and emotionally fragile people with Saturn in the watery signs can be. They need constant reassurance. They desperately long for intimacy and yet at the same time they are afraid of it. The watery Saturn

People with Saturn in a Water sign can be emotionally
fragile, needing a lot of reassurance and nourishment.

type has learned as a child that to ask for love
and to be open to receive it is to risk suffering
and pain.

If you have Venus in an earthy sign, the
gift you can give to these grown-up children
is that of stability, grounding, and the moth-
ering quality that they are unconsciously
looking for. Your task won't be easy but it
will certainly be very
rewarding .

VENUS IN TAURUS
— What we have just said
is especially applicable to
those with Venus in Taurus.
Your watery Saturn partner is
not looking for just sex and/or power in his
love life — excitement and passion may interest him for a while, but not for long. He needs
real emotional nourishment and he knows it.
He will not open up, or stop changing his
partners, until he finds the person who can
provide it. With Venus in Taurus you can be
that person. This will be your gift to him:
your motherly instincts, your compassion,
and your warm, benevolent openness.

What you should avoid: make sure that
your presence doesn't become a kind of
addiction, something he cannot live without.
He needs to be loved and reassured, but he
also needs to be challenged to grow and to
stand on his own feet.

VENUS IN VIRGO — The attraction
between you is likely to be very strong, as is
often the case between polar
opposites. When you love,
you never let your feelings
alone determine your
behavior, nor will you
ever turn against your
own interests and
well-being. You never let
your heart rule over your
intelligence and common sense: you try to
find a balance between them. Those who have
Saturn in Water find it very difficult to
achieve this kind of emotional equilibrium,
without loving help from another. They are
prone either to repress their feelings with an
iron hand (and consequently become prey to
all kinds of psychosomatic illnesses) or to set
aside prudence and rationality only to end up
in destructive sometimes masochistic love
affairs. Your gift will consist in teaching your
partner how not to be self-destructive, how to

Venus in Taurus brings simplicity, gentleness and
harmony not as abstract ideas but as natural,
everyday experiences.

make friends with his own feeling nature. What you should avoid: remember that you are not a nurse.

VENUS IN CAPRICORN — You are a powerful person and your partner is probably just as powerful as you are. If the feeling between you is strong and sincere, or if you want it to grow in that direction, remember: nobody can claim any strength who hasn't dared to expose the wounds of his heart, who doesn't know how to make himself vulnerable. You have a willingness to take responsibility for all that is wrong in your love life, and to do something about it. This gift will have a serious, almost "paternal" quality about it, since you go for the substance of things and don't try to look lovable or sweet.

What you should avoid: when it comes to lowering the defenses, never demand that it should be the other who takes the first step.

Venus in an Earth Sign
MEETING WITH
Saturn in an Earth Sign

As we know from above, Saturn in an Earth sign brings a need to grow roots not only in the material world but also, and especially, inside one's own being. In matters of love, the situations that arise with the Hard Master of Love in an Earth sign are easy to recognize. Here is the man who sacrifices his emotional life in favor of the struggle to accumulate more and more money, for example. This is the person who brings into his relationships the crippling belief that money can buy everything, even affection. Or the woman who values material things (clothes, jewelry, houses, or the beauty of her own body) more than anything else, and who invariably falls in love with men who bring not fun and adventure into her life, but only material comfort. In any case, the mistake here is always the same: that of attaching too much value to material things rather than to qualities or "states of being" such as real love.

Those who focus on the material alone are in fact trying to avoid deeper, more challenging realities. Venus in the earthy signs can help them confront these realities.

An earthy Venus can prove a perfect match for Saturn in an Earth sign, because it brings together the different principles of the planet Venus (love, feelings, emotions) and of

An earthy Venus can prove a perfect match for an earthy Saturn, because they can bring together the different principles of Earth in a nourishing, harmonious way.

the element Earth (the world, the body, material objects) in a nourishing and harmonious way.

VENUS IN TAURUS can create an aura of serenity and affection which spreads through every aspect of her relationship.

If you have Venus in Taurus, simplicity, gentleness, and harmony are not abstract ideas but natural, everyday experiences. In the eyes of an earthy Saturn partner you appear like a dream come true: a woman who is able to love him for what he is, not for what he has; a person who knows how to take care of him.

What you should avoid: jealousy and possessiveness.

VENUS IN VIRGO offers a detached, balanced, and grounded approach to life in all its facets. Your gift will be the ability to show your partner that in love there is really no higher and no lower. Being useful to somebody, "serving" him, is a beautiful experience when you do it out of a free, deliberate, loving choice.

VENUS IN CAPRICORN — You are not likely to fall in love with people who have no courage or self-respect. That's why if you are interested in a man with Saturn in an Earth sign you will stimulate what is best in him: the people you feel an affinity with need to prove their worth in the eyes of others, in a tangible way.

What you should avoid: make sure that your love, help and devotion are directed to the person and not to the power that he wields, or is trying to achieve.

Venus in an Earth Sign
MEETING WITH
Saturn in an Air Sign
(Gemini, Libra, Aquarius)

The earthy Venus who wants to reach the heart of an airy Saturn will have to give a new scope to her practical, concrete wisdom. She will have to create a common ground of loving understanding between herself and her partner.

If you can protect your lover from your own
possessiveness, you will also benefit, because a free lover
is much happier than a caged one.

Her gift will be to accept and encourage his need to communicate. Airy Saturn needs to speak and define facts and feelings much more than this Venus does. For an earthy Venus, the facts convey all that needs to be said, for she tends to express herself in a very practical way. If she can recognize this difference between herself and her partner, and bridge it, she will not only win his affection but also his gratitude.

VENUS IN TAURUS — Your natural optimism will be the best medicine for your lover's innate pessimism. Your special gift will consist in showing him that aloneness and lack of communication are really a choice, not an inescapable destiny. You are a very beautiful and lovable person and you can give much to your beloved. Make sure every little thing you give is given along with some affectionate word: this will help him to open his heart as well, for he needs to find words to express his feelings.

What you should avoid: in most cases it is quite easy to keep a lover with an airy Saturn all for yourself; deep down he feels lonely and it is natural for him to cling to you (unless he is the kind who chooses to overre-

act against his fears and limitations and become distant and aloof). But remember that he needs to be open to other people as well, not just to you. If you can protect him from your own possessiveness you will also benefit, because a free lover is much happier than a caged one.

VENUS IN VIRGO — A person with Saturn in an Air sign is likely to be interested in you because he will feel some kind of affinity with you, and yet a stimulating difference. Just like him, you tend to be moderate and rather prudent in matters of love: you like to start slowly and keep going till the end. You are not glamorous, but you have that kind of shy grace he finds all the more appealing because it is neither pretentious nor intimidating. Even when other people are around, you know how to make him feel he's the one you are really interested in, which is the kind of reassurance he needs. He never feels really at ease in any kind of social situation, and seldom trusts his own intelligence and ability to communicate.

The situation for you is quite different. Wherever you are it is not difficult for you to fit in. You are not interested in the limelight;

Of the three Air signs, Gemini is the most playful one.
You may wonder why your partner can't simply relax
and take things as they come!

you accept the place you are given without resentment or pride. You are intelligent enough to know that sooner or later your merits will be recognized: you don't need either to hide them or to exaggerate them. Your gift to the airy Saturn will be to help him discover his potential and to find his place in society. What you should avoid: being right all the time. It will drive him crazy.

VENUS IN CAPRICORN — If you have Venus in Capricorn your honesty and sincerity are what your Saturnine partner will love and respect most in you, since neither of you believes in the motto, "all who love are blind." In you he will find no concession to social acceptability, or even fashionable lies: you respect yourself too much to bow to others' prejudices and expectations. You believe in being totally honest about what you are ready to give and what you expect in exchange. For you, a relationship is not only a romance but also a contract. Honesty and sincerity are your gifts.

What you should avoid: being too uncompromising, too aggressive about planning both your futures and setting down the rules.

Venus in an Air Sign
(Gemini, Libra, Aquarius)
MEETING WITH
Saturn in a Fire Sign
(Aries, Leo, Sagittarius)

For people with Venus in one of the airy signs there is no question of "falling" — they "rise" in love. Whatever their actual age may be, their hearts will always be young and light, and will never tie them down to the ground. For them, love has much in common with friendship; it is a pleasant and gratifying experience, but nothing to lose sleep over.

The gift of Venus in an Air sign to the tormented fiery Saturn partner is a very innocent and playful one: "If you want to be with me, forget about drama — let's have fun together!"

VENUS IN GEMINI — Of the three airy signs, Gemini is the most playful one. If you have this Venus and you are interested in someone with Saturn in Fire, you probably cannot understand why such a beautiful man wastes so much energy in brooding and gives himself such a hard time. You wonder why your partner can't simply relax and take things as they come. In any case when you

For people with Venus in one of the Air signs there is no question of "falling"—they "rise" in love.

are together you are quite happy with your "one man show": you like being the center of attention and for this, a silent partner is a help! Your gift will be your sense of humor. Saturn in Fire is too identified with his problems to be talked into dropping his fears. But if you can make him laugh you stand a good chance to reach his heart.

What you should avoid: make sure he understands your jokes, and never gets the impression that you are making fun of him.

VENUS IN LIBRA — Your partner will be able to trust you more than anybody else, because "love" for you means in the first place respect for the other's individuality. However different he may be from what you would like him to be, you will never try to change him according to your desires. As time goes by he will realize the sincerity of your intentions and he will appreciate you more and more.

Your gift is a cool and detached kind of affection which doesn't demand that the other should first be worthy of it.

What you should avoid: that your tolerance and objectivity slip into indifference.

VENUS IN AQUARIUS — You are not the kind of person who can be happy with a routine of a sleepy but comfortable relationship. At core you are an idealist, and you believe that love should be an ever-changing experience full of creativity, freedom and enthusiasm. In fact, you are not interested in love as sex, passion and possessiveness: what you are looking for is a higher love, something which can give meaning to your life.

The partner with Saturn in one of the fiery signs is actually looking for the same experience: something deep and spiritual enough to rekindle the fire of his soul. Your gift is to share your creativity and sense of adventure.

What you should avoid: don't ask too much from yourself or from him. Real people are more important than the most beautiful ideal.

Venus in an Air sign meeting Saturn in a Water sign will probably find that as far as the heart is concerned the two of you belong to different worlds.

Venus in an Air Sign
MEETING WITH
Saturn in a Water Sign
(Cancer, Scorpio, Pisces)

If you have Venus in one of the airy signs and you are interested in a person with Saturn in a Water sign, you will probably find that as far as the heart is concerned the two of you are speaking different languages and belong to different worlds. In love, you look for an experience that makes your life more interesting and exciting. The worst that can happen to you is boredom. The watery Saturn needs stability and constant reassurance, and is ready to sacrifice everything for it. He is trying to get the emotional nourishment he missed when he was child. Yet, a meeting can happen, because sometimes the heart is stirred to action rather than discouraged by obstacles. Don't be blind to the obstacles, but remember that between lovers there are no differences that sincere feelings cannot bridge.

VENUS IN GEMINI — Beware of your tendency to express yourself in a humorous

Don't be blind to the obstacles, but remember that
between lovers there are no differences that sincere
feelings cannot bridge.

way. You don't mean any harm, but your
partner's heart is still bleeding from old
wounds that he is trying his best to cover up:
you might, unknowingly, expose them again.
And when you are in the company of others
and you feel at your best, remember to give
some attention to your lover as well. A look
or a smile will be enough if your heart is
behind it. But he will never forgive you if you
forget him completely, even if it is just for a
few hours during a party.

Your gift to him is in your smile: it can give
your lover the feeling that with you, he really
has a chance to let go of his past forever.

What you should avoid: thinking that you
can solve all problems by not taking them
seriously.

VENUS IN LIBRA — Your tolerant attitude toward the whims and unreasonable
behavior of your partner is likely to be misunderstood as indifference. As far as you are
concerned, to love someone means to be able
to take him the way he is. But you are missing
one important point: in behaving the way he
does, your watery Saturn is testing your reac-
tions. He is trying to provoke the emotional
response he needs in order to feel loved.

Remember the watery Saturn needs kisses, hugs and
tender sex more than charming words.

Your gift to him will be your maturity, and also your willingness to go out of your way to understand him.

What you should avoid: doing your fingernails when he is breaking down, or being the loving angel when he needs to be yelled at.

VENUS IN AQUARIUS — Your attachment to friends and your idealistic conception of love can put you into trouble with your watery Saturn lover. He needs kisses, hugs, warmth, and tender sex more than the most poetic and charming words. And he would rather be alone with you than to be introduced to all of your friends.

Your gift to him will be the enthusiasm with which you greet every new day.

What you should avoid: feeling hurt when he doesn't understand you. You can be just as impossible!

Venus in an Air Sign
MEETING WITH
Saturn in an Earth Sign
(Taurus, Virgo, Capricorn)

If you invest too much in the material world (Saturn in Earth) you may earn power and prestige, but you will miss out on love, happiness, and peace of mind. Venus in Air represents love for beauty, for freedom, for playfulness — and that is what she will bring to her lover, rescuing him from the living death of a purely material existence.

VENUS IN GEMINI — You are like a fresh breeze in the life of the person you choose to be with. When you are in love you feel much younger than your real age. You like action, good company, music; you are always ready to go out and enjoy yourself. You will bring a real injection of optimism and energy for your Saturnine partner. Before meeting you, he probably always thought that laughter was silly and having fun was unbecoming to a serious and important person. In your company he will have to change his mind: you like to have a good time, but are far from superficial. Love gives you a grace and a lightness that your beloved secretly admires.

What you should avoid: don't forget the distinction between being innocent, fresh and childlike, and being irresponsible and childish.

VENUS IN LIBRA — Moral beauty is one of the qualities you appreciate most. In your

Don't be too harsh in your judgments. Be ready to
forgive... or, better, to pretend that you have not seen.

partner you value an attractive appearance,
but also the kind of refined inner beauty
which is the reflection of a life lived intensely
and sincerely. Saturn in his earthy placement
gives an austere grace to those who take
every setback as a chance to grow more loving and wise. This is the kind of person with
whom you are likely to forge a lasting relationship.

Your gift to the relationship will be that of
faithfulness and commitment. You will
respect your partner and he will respect you.

What you should avoid: don't be too harsh
in your judgments. Be ready to forgive... or,
better, to pretend that you have not seen.

VENUS IN AQUARIUS — Your love for
freedom will probably be a challenge and a
hard test for your partner. Saturn in Earth
brings a tendency to want to own, to dominate. If your partner is rich, he will probably
try to "buy" you in order to keep you in his
control. If he is one who looks down on
wealth, or has failed to achieve it, his possessiveness will be less apparent but all the more
obstinate and unaware.

Your gift to him will be to help him grow
as an independent individual by not letting

him cling to you. Only when he stops trying
to control the people he loves will he also be
free.

What you should avoid: Don't overlook
the distinction between being independent
and being afraid of committing yourself.

Venus in an Air Sign
MEETING WITH
Saturn in an Air Sign

The meeting of an airy Venus and an airy
Saturn is a rare and fortunate event, when it
is not just a superficial acquaintance or a flir-
tation. More often than not, the airy Saturn
will admire his luckier acquaintance from a
distance, appreciating her wit, her charming
manners, her circle of friends, her originality,
and her ability to love without clinging. In
comparison he might feel unintelligent and
boring, a victim not a winner. This one is not
likely to make the first move, and the other
will be unlikely to give him a second look.
But if the meeting does happen the partnership will bear beautiful fruit.

If you have Venus in one of the airy signs,
your love and your presence will help your

If you have Venus in one of the Air signs, your love and
your presence will help your lover to open up, to trust
his own intelligence, to be more lighthearted.

lover to open up to other people, to trust his own intelligence, and to be more lighthearted and less pessimistic. And on the other side, he will challenge you to acknowledge the darker side of things, to be less superficial and more loving.

VENUS IN GEMINI — You can count on your intellectual charm to win your beloved's admiration. You need not do anything special to make him fall in love with you: slowly, slowly (he doesn't like to be rushed) take him into your life. He will love it: you are what he always wanted to be, totally at ease. You live an interesting life; share it with him.

Your gift will consist in making your beloved feel as special as you do. What you should avoid: if you are living together, don't complain if you cannot go out every night!

VENUS IN LIBRA — The experiences of your airy Saturn partner have very likely been difficult ones: betrayals, desertions, loneliness... No wonder he has lost all trust in love! With Venus in Libra you are a person whose fidelity and commitment are beyond doubt when you really care for someone. You don't like to deceive or to play with the feelings of others. You can be the one who can

bring your partner a renewed hope in the possibility of love.

Your gift will be your offer of a relationship based on mutual trust and mature choice, in which you never take him for granted.

What you should avoid: waiting too long before saying yes.

VENUS IN AQUARIUS — Conformism is your worst enemy, but people with Saturn in an Air sign do tend to be conformists. They are afraid of being disapproved of and left alone, so they rarely allow themselves to be too open with their friends and lovers. But, inside, they actually hate to conform as much as you do! In a love relationship you will be able to wake up the social rebel in him, the one who is ready to risk his respectability and social approval for the sake of truth. People might say that he has lost his head over you, and that he is going to be sorry. But he will know that he has never been so happy before. This will be your gift to him, to free him from the fear of "what people might say."

What you should avoid: deserting him when he is taking risks!

STONE		PROPERTIES	MAGICAL USES	PAGE
	MOONSTONE	Stone of the Moon. Helps to get acquainted with the Moon.	To meet your Lunar Ally. For a date with destiny.	28 24
	PINK QUARTZ	The healing stone. Heals heart and body. Purifies implements and furniture.	To heal love wounds.	196
	PEARL	The stone of womanhood and mystery. For lasting love.	On the love altar. For woman's magic philtre.	49 164
	DIAMOND	Everlasting love.	On the love altar.	49
	GARNET	The stone of sexual pleasure and sensuality.	On the love altar. To awaken the body to sensuality. To raise sexual potential.	49 178 193
	JADE	The stone of the body. Brings beauty and health.	Bathroom altar. For your beauty to surface.	191
	BLUE LACED AGATE	To open your heart to love. Brings softness. Makes you vulnerable again.	To open your heart to love.	179
	EMERALD	To know the truth about a situation. To help self-expression.	Jealousy magic. To decide upon a commitment. For a choice in love.	185 201
	RUBY	The stone of a "high voltage" love affair, passion, union, deep and gratifying.	For a lover to appear in your life.	183

Stones for Love Magic

Bruno Kortenhorst and Carlos Rios

2/3, 6, 7, 8, 15, 22/23, 24, 28 to 50/51, 56, 57, 58, 59, 60, 62, 62/63, 64, 66/67, 72, 73, 74/75, 77, 79, 83, 85, 86, 89, 90, 95, 97, 98/99, 99, 106, 106/107, 110, 113, 114/115, 116, 118/119, 121, 123, 125, 126, 132/133, 134, 138, 139, 142, 145, 146, 147, 148, 150, 152/153, 155, 156, 159, 160, 162, 165, 167, 170/171 to 185, 189, 190/191, 194, 195, 198, 198/199, 200, 202, 203, 204, 206/207, 207, 214/215, 218, 221, 226, 231, 239, 240, 241, 242, 246 (moonstone, pink quartz, diamond, jade, blue laced agate), 247, 249

Carmen Strider

26/27, 46, 68, 80, 246 (pearls, garnet, emerald, ruby)

Fine Art Photographs

Jan Breughel: 82/83, 86/87, 90/91, 94/95

Inter Ikea Systems B.V.

54/55, 61, 65

Images

De Sphaera: 127, 222

K&B News

A. Vergari: 25

Le Louvre

Théodore Chasseriau: 71

Pictor International

18/19, 21, 124/125

The Bridgeman Art Library

Alma-Tadema: 70

The Wallace Collection

Fragonard: 10/11
Greuze: 12
Watteau: 69
Mayer: 78/79
Poussin: 186/187

Random House UK Limited

The A. E. Waite tarot cards.

Dover

Pictorial Archive of Decorative Renaissance Woodcuts: 13

Acknowledgments

DIARY

DATE	MOON PHASE	RISING TIME	SETTING TIME	ASTRO SIGN	ELEMENT	COLOR	STONE	MAGIC RITUAL

DIARY

DATE	MOON PHASE	RISING TIME	SETTING TIME	ASTRO SIGN	ELEMENT	COLOR	STONE	MAGIC RITUAL

DIARY

DATE	MOON PHASE	RISING TIME	SETTING TIME	ASTRO SIGN	ELEMENT	COLOR	STONE	MAGIC RITUAL

DIARY

DATE	MOON PHASE	RISING TIME	SETTING TIME	ASTRO SIGN	ELEMENT	COLOR	STONE	MAGIC RITUAL

DATE	MOON PHASE	RISING TIME	SETTING TIME	ASTRO SIGN	ELEMENT	COLOR	STONE	MAGIC RITUAL

DIARY

DATE	MOON PHASE	RISING TIME	SETTING TIME	ASTRO SIGN	ELEMENT	COLOR	STONE	MAGIC RITUAL

DIARY

DATE	MOON PHASE	RISING TIME	SETTING TIME	ASTRO SIGN	ELEMENT	COLOR	STONE	MAGIC RITUAL